"十三五"职业教育规划教材
高职高专汽车专业"互联网+"创新规划教材

# 汽车专业英语图解教程
# （第2版）

主　编　侯锁军　王旭东
副主编　胡　桦　陈海燕

## 内 容 简 介

本书以汽车构造知识为基础，主要包括汽车构造、发动机构造、曲柄连杆机构、配气机构、汽油发动机燃油供给系统、汽油发动机点火系统、汽油发动机计算机辅助控制系统、柴油发动机燃料供给系统、汽车冷却系统、发动机润滑系统、发动机起动系统、汽车传动系统、汽车行驶系统、汽车转向系统、汽车制动系统、汽车电气系统、汽车空调系统及汽车维修工具和设备等内容。全书分为18个单元，每个单元包括中英文对照的结构图或原理图、阅读材料及译文。本书内容翔实新颖、图文并茂、深入浅出、通俗易懂。

本书可以作为高等工程专科学校、高等职业技术学校汽车检测与维修专业、汽车制造与装配专业、汽车电子技术专业以及汽车技术服务与营销专业等汽车类相关专业学生的教材，又可供汽车维修和汽车销售等相关专业人员自学和参考。

### 图书在版编目（CIP）数据

汽车专业英语图解教程/侯锁军，王旭东主编．—2版．—北京：北京大学出版社，2016.3
（高职高专汽车专业"互联网+"创新规划教材）
ISBN 978-7-301-26595-6

Ⅰ.①汽… Ⅱ.①侯… ②王… Ⅲ.①汽车工程—英语—高等职业教育—教材 Ⅳ.①H31

中国版本图书馆CIP数据核字(2015)第293455号

| | |
|---|---|
| 书　　　　名 | 汽车专业英语图解教程（第2版）<br>Qiche Zhuanye Yingyu Tujie Jiaocheng |
| 著作责任者 | 侯锁军　王旭东　主编 |
| 策划编辑 | 刘晓东 |
| 责任编辑 | 翟　源 |
| 数字编辑 | 刘志秀 |
| 标准书号 | ISBN 978-7-301-26595-6 |
| 出版发行 | 北京大学出版社 |
| 地　　　　址 | 北京市海淀区成府路205号　100871 |
| 网　　　　址 | http://www.pup.cn　新浪微博:@北京大学出版社 |
| 电子信箱 | pup_6@163.com |
| 电　　　　话 | 邮购部 62752015　发行部 62750672　编辑部 62750667 |
| 印　刷　者 | 北京溢漾印刷有限公司 |
| 经　销　者 | 新华书店 |
| | 787毫米×1092毫米　16开本　11.25印张　260千字<br>2010年9月第1版<br>2016年3月第2版　2018年8月第4次印刷 |
| 定　　　　价 | 29.00元 |

未经许可，不得以任何方式复制或抄袭本书之部分或全部内容。
**版权所有，侵权必究**
举报电话：010-62752024　电子信箱：fd@pup.pku.edu.cn
图书如有印装质量问题，请与出版部联系，电话：010-62756370

# 前 言

职业教育是国民教育体系的重要组成部分,是广大青年打开通往成功成才大门的重要途径。本书结合高职高专汽车专业人才培养模式和现代汽车市场需求编写而成,旨在使汽车专业学生成为既懂汽车专业知识又知晓汽车专业英语的专门人才。

本书改变传统的汽车专业英语编写方法,通过图解的方式对汽车各系统的结构进行专业英文解释,使汽车各系统的结构名称与专业词汇一一对应,目的是帮助学生更快、更好地掌握英语专业词汇。本书还提供了阅读材料,加强学生阅读和翻译汽车专业英文资料的能力,以便更好地从国外资料中汲取先进的汽车科技知识。

本书由侯锁军和王旭东任主编,胡桦和陈海燕任副主编,具体编写分工如下:新乡医学院三全学院胡桦编写第1、2、3、4、5、6单元,河南机电高等专科学校王旭东编写第7、8、9、10单元以及附录部分,河南职业技术学院陈海燕编写第11、12、13单元,河南机电高等专科学校侯锁军编写第14、15、16、17、18单元。全书由侯锁军统稿。

本书建议安排30~40学时进行学习,各院校教师可根据不同的专业设置灵活安排。

由于时间仓促,编写水平有限,书中难免存在不足之处,恳请读者批评指正。

编　者
2015年10月

# 目　录

Unit 1　STRUCTURE OF AUTOMOBILE　汽车构造 ………………………………………… 1
Unit 2　STRUCTURE OF ENGINE　发动机构造 …………………………………………… 7
Unit 3　CRANKSHAFT-CONNECTING ROD MECHANISM　曲柄连杆机构 …………… 16
Unit 4　VALVE TRAIN　配气机构 …………………………………………………………… 25
Unit 5　FUEL SUPPLY SYSTEM FOR GASOLINE ENGINE　汽油发动机燃油供给系统 …… 33
Unit 6　GASOLINE ENGINE IGNITION SYSTEM　汽油发动机点火系统 ……………… 44
Unit 7　GASOLINE ENGINE COMPUTER-AIDED CONTROL SYSTEM
　　　　汽油发动机计算机辅助控制系统 …………………………………………………… 51
Unit 8　FUEL SUPPLY SYSTEM FOR DIESEL ENGINE　柴油发动机燃料供给系统 …… 64
Unit 9　AUTOMOBILE COOLING SYSTEM　汽车冷却系统 …………………………… 74
Unit 10　ENGINE LUBRICATION SYSTEM　发动机润滑系统 ………………………… 80
Unit 11　ENGINE STARTING SYSTEM　发动机起动系统 ……………………………… 86
Unit 12　AUTOMOBILE POWER TRAIN　汽车传动系统 ……………………………… 93
Unit 13　AUTOMOBILE RUNNING GEAR　汽车行驶系统 ……………………………… 106
Unit 14　AUTOMOBILE STEERING SYSTEM　汽车转向系统 ………………………… 115
Unit 15　AUTOMOBILE BRAKE SYSTEM　汽车制动系统 ……………………………… 125
Unit 16　AUTOMOBILE ELECTRICAL SYSTEM　汽车电气系统 ……………………… 136
Unit 17　AUTOMOBILE AIR CONDITIONING SYSTEM　汽车空调系统 ……………… 143
Unit 18　AUTOMOBILE REPAIR TOOLS AND EQUIPMENTS　汽车维修工具和设备 …… 150
附录 A　汽车专业词汇（英—汉）……………………………………………………………… 157
附录 B　汽车专业英语常见名词缩写 ………………………………………………………… 166
参考文献 ………………………………………………………………………………………… 172

# Unit 1

# STRUCTURE OF AUTOMOBILE
# 汽车构造

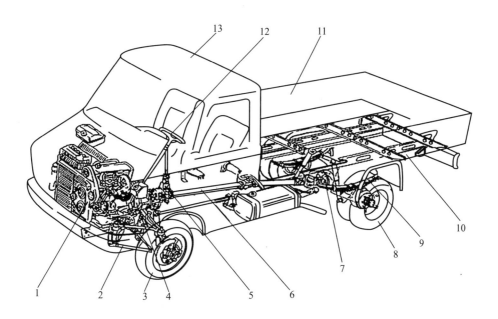

图 1.1　General structure of automobile　汽车的总体构造

1—engine 发动机；2—front suspension 前悬架；3—steering vehicle wheel 转向车轮；
4—clutch 离合器；5—transmission 变速器；6—universal transmission device
万向传动装置；7—drive-axle 驱动桥；8—driving wheel 驱动车轮；
9—rear suspension 后悬架；10—frame 车架；
11—carriage 车厢；12—steering wheel
转向盘；13—cab 驾驶室

【参考图文】

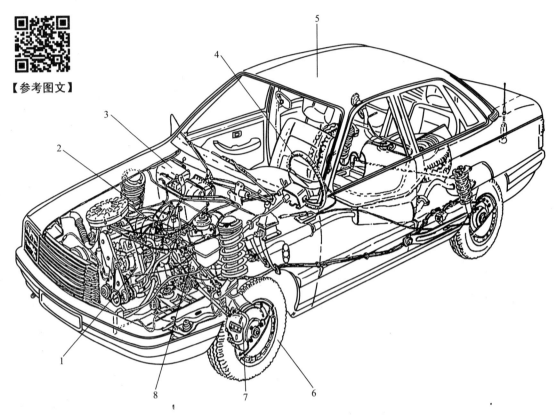

图 1.2  Structure of passenger car  乘用车的总体构造

1—engine 发动机；2—suspension system 悬架；3—air conditioner 空调；4—steering wheel 转向盘；
5—body 车身；6—driving wheel 驱动车轮；7—brake 制动器；8—transmission 变速器

## Reading Materials

### Passage 1

#### Structure of Automobile

Today's car contains more than 15,000 separate, individual parts that must work together. These parts can be grouped into four major categories: engine, chassis, body and electrical system.

#### Engine

Today, the four-stroke cycle internal combustion engines are commonly used in cars, trucks, motorcycles and many other transport vehicles. The four strokes refer to intake, compression, combustion and exhaust strokes that occur during two crankshaft rotations per working cycle of Otto Cycle.

The engine provides power to move the automobile. The most common type of automotive engine is the gasoline-burning engine. It is found in most automobiles.

Diesel-fuel burning engines are also used in modern passenger cars, as well as in large trucks. All engines have fuel, exhaust, cooling, and lubrication systems. Gasoline engines also have an ignition system.

### Chassis

A chassis which is considered as a support frame for an auto body is used to assemble all auto spare parts on it. In fact, when power from engine continues to be transmitted to chassis, it begins with power train, and goes on to steering, wheel suspension, brakes and tires. These individual components interact with each other closely.

### Body

The automobile body which is regarded as the framework is seated on the chassis. Its function is obvious for occupants to provide comfort, protection and shelter. The automobile body is generally divided into five sections: the front, the upper, the top, the rear and the underbody. Theses sections are further divided into small units, such as the hood, the fender, the roof panels, the door, the instrument panel, the bumpers and the luggage compartment.

### The Electrical System

The electrical system is considered as an auto electric power source supplying lighting power for the automobile. The electrical system contains battery, lights, generator, engine ignition, lighting circuit, and various switches that control their use.

## 阅读材料

**材料1（参考译文）**

### 汽车构造

如今，每辆汽车平均包含15 000多个各自独立而又必须共同作用的零部件。这些零部件可分为四大类：发动机、底盘、车身和电气系统。

**发动机**

目前，轿车、货车、摩托车和其他车辆采用的发动机通常是四冲程内燃机。四个冲程是指在一个奥托循环周期内，曲轴转两圈活塞完成进气行程、压缩行程、做功行程和排气行程。

发动机提供动力使汽车行驶。汽车发动机最常见的类型是汽油发动机，大多数汽车采用这种发动机。柴油发动机也用在现代乘用车以及大型载货车上。所有的发动机均包括燃油系统、排气系统、冷却系统和润滑系统。汽油发动机还包括点火系统。

**底盘**

底盘被认为是一个支撑车身的框架，用来组装汽车上所有的零部件。事实上，当从发动机产生的动力连续不断地传送到底盘时，它从传动系开始，接着传递到转向系统、车轮悬挂、制动系统和轮胎。这些单个组件相互密切合作，完成汽车行驶。

### 车身

车身是固定在底盘上的框架。它的功能明显是为乘客提供舒适的环境、保护和庇护。汽车车身一般分为五个部分：前部、上部、顶部、后部和底部。这些部分又被进一步分为更小的单元，如发动机盖、挡泥板、车顶板、车门、仪表板、保险杠和行李箱等。

### 电气系统

电气系统是汽车的电源供应装置，用于向汽车照明系统提供电能。电气系统包括蓄电池、指示灯、发电机、发动机点火系统、照明电路和控制其使用的各种开关。

## Passage 2

### Automotive Industry

The global automotive industry is a highly diversified sector that comprises of manufacturers, suppliers, dealers, retailers, original equipment manufacturers, aftermarket parts manufacturers, automotive engineers, motor mechanics, auto electricians, spray painters or body repairers, fuel producers, environmental and transport safety groups, and trade unions.

The automobile and automotive parts & components manufacturers constitute a major chunk of automotive industry throughout the world. The automotive manufacturing sector consists of automobile and light truck manufacturers, motor vehicle body manufacturers, and motor vehicle parts and supplies manufacturers. This sector is engaged in manufacturing of automotive and light duty motor vehicles, motor vehicle bodies, chassis, cabs, trucks, automobile and utility trailers, buses, military vehicles, and motor vehicle gasoline engines.

### The Top Auto-making Nations

The United States, Japan, China, Germany and Republic of Korea are the top five automobile manufacturing nations throughout the world. The United States is the world's largest producer and consumer of motor vehicles, automobiles accounting for 6.6 million direct and spin-off jobs and representing nearly 10% of the $10 trillion US economy. Automobile is one of the important industries in the world, which provides employment to 25 million people in the world.

In the recent past, the auto parts manufacturing industry of Midwest lost 12.7% of its employment. The various factors behind this decline are unemployment recession, domestic relocation and foreign competition. This loss in employment has badly affected this industry.

### Major Manufacturing Regions

Northeastern United States and Southern Great Lakes Region, Northwestern Europe,

# Unit 1　STRUCTURE OF AUTOMOBILE

Western Russia and Ukraine, and Japan are the major manufacturing regions of automobile in the world. In North America, the prominent automotive manufacturing regions are New England, New York and the Mid-Atlantic, Central New York, Pittsburgh/Cleveland, Western Great Lakes, St. Lawrence Valley, Ohio and Eastern Indiana, Kanawha and middle Ohio Valley, St. Louis, the Southeastern region, Gulf Coast, Central Florida, and the West Coast. The European Union has the largest automotive production regions in the World. The key automobile manufacturing regions are United Kingdom, Rhine-Ruhr River Valley, Upper Rhine-Alsace-Lorraine region, and the Po Valley in Italy.

In the Western Russia and Ukraine, the leading industrial regions are Moscow, the Ukraine region, the Volga region and the Urals regions.

### Major Industry Players

The worldwide automobile industry is largely dominated by five leading automobile manufacturing corporations namely Toyota, General Motors, Ford Motor Company, Volkswagen AG, and Daimler Chrysler. These corporations have their presence in almost every country and they continue to invest into production facilities in emerging markets namely Latin America, Middle East, Eastern Europe, China, Malaysia and other markets in Southeast Asia with the main aim of reducing their production costs.

## 材料2（参考译文）

### 汽　车　行　业

全球汽车业是一个高度多样化的行业，包括制造商、供应商、经销商、零售商、原始设备制造商、售后服务零部件制造商、汽车工程师、汽车维修师、汽车电工、喷绘师和汽车维修人员、燃料生产商、环境和安全运输集团、贸易联盟。

汽车和汽车零部件生产商是整个汽车行业的主要组成部分。汽车制造业由汽车制造商、汽车车身制造商和汽车零部件供应商构成。该行业涉及轻型汽车、汽车车身、底盘、驾驶室、卡车、轿车和公共拖车、公共汽车、军用车辆以及汽车汽油发动机的生产制造。

### 顶级汽车制造国

美国、日本、中国、德国和韩国是世界五大汽车生产国。美国是世界上最大的汽车制造和汽车消费国，其汽车业提供660万个直接和间接的工作岗位，并占美国10万亿经济总额的近10%。汽车是世界重要的产业之一，它为世界上2500万人提供了就业岗位。

在过去的几年中，中西部地区的汽车零部件制造行业失去12.7%的就业岗位，其主要原因是经济衰退、国内迁移和国外竞争，就业率的下降已严重影响了美国汽车业。

### 主要生产地区

美国的东北部和南部大湖地区、欧洲西北部地区、俄罗斯的西部地区和乌克兰以及日本是世界上主要的汽车制造地区。在北美，优势突出的汽车制造地区是新英格兰、纽约和大西洋中部、纽约中部、匹兹堡/克利夫兰、西部大湖区、圣劳伦斯河谷、俄亥俄州和印第安纳州东部、俄亥俄河谷和中卡纳瓦、圣路易斯、东南地区、墨西哥湾、佛罗里达州中部和西部海岸。欧盟在世界拥有最大的汽车生产地区,其主要的汽车制造业地区是英国、莱茵河流域、鲁尔河流域、莱茵河上游—阿尔萨斯—洛林地区和意大利波河流域。

在俄罗斯西部和乌克兰,主要工业地区是莫斯科、乌克兰地区、伏尔加地区、乌拉尔地区。

**主要行业主导者**

全球汽车业在很大程度上被五大汽车制造公司所主导,即丰田汽车公司、通用汽车公司、福特汽车公司、大众汽车公司和戴姆勒·克莱斯勒汽车公司。这些公司几乎遍及每个国家,它们不遗余力地在新兴市场投入生产设施,即拉丁美洲、中东、东欧、中国、马来西亚和其他东南亚市场,主要目的是降低生产成本。

# Unit 2

# STRUCTURE OF ENGINE
# 发动机构造

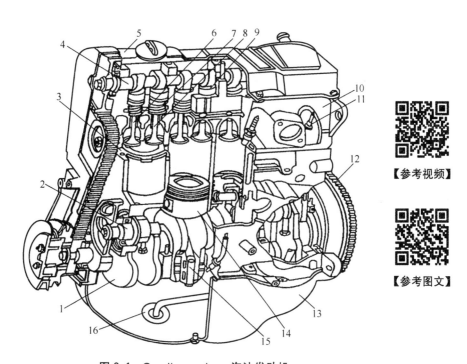

图 2.1　Gasoline engine　汽油发动机

1—crankshaft 曲轴；2—intermediate shaft 中间轴；3—cylinder block 气缸体；
4—camshaft 凸轮轴；5—camshaft cover 凸轮轴罩盖；6—exhaust valve 排气门；
7—valve spring 气门弹簧；8—intake valve 进气门；9—tappet 气门挺杆；
10—cylinder 气缸；11—spark plug 火花塞；12—flywheel 飞轮；
13—oil pan 油底盘；14—piston 活塞；
15—connecting rod assembly 连杆总成；
16—oil strainer 机油滤网

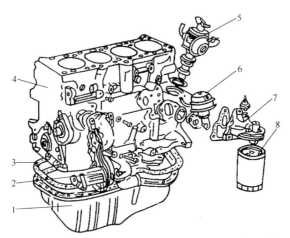

图 2.2　Main accessories of gasoline engine　汽油发动机的主要附件
1—oil pan 油底盘；2—pump 水泵；3—sealing gasket 密封垫；4—cylinder block 气缸体；
5—distributor 分电器；6—gas filter 汽油滤清器；7—gas filter installation seat 机油滤清器安装座；
8—oil filter 机油滤清器

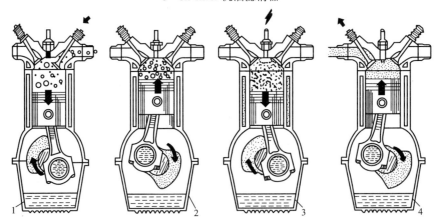

图 2.3　Operational schematic of single cylinder four-stroke engine　单缸四冲程汽油发动机工作原理
1—intake stroke 进气行程；2—compression stroke 压缩行程；
3—power stroke 做功行程；4—exhaust stroke 排气行程

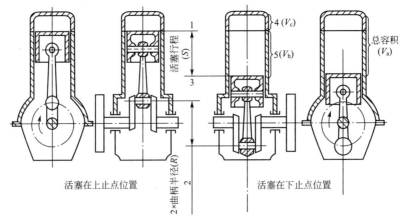

图 2.4　Basic term of engine　发动机基本术语
1—top dead center 上止点；2—long stroke 活塞行程；3—bottom dead center 下止点；
4—volume of combustion chamber 燃烧室容积；5—working volume 工作容积

# Unit 2  STRUCTURE OF ENGINE

## Reading Materials

### Passage 1

#### Kinds of Engines

The engine is the heart of an automobile. The purpose of an automotive engine is to convert fuel into the energy that moves the automobile. Currently the easiest way to create motion from fuel is to burn the fuel inside an engine. Therefore, an automotive engine is an internal combustion engine, which burns fuel within the cylinders and converts the expanding force of the combustion into rotary force used to drive the automobile.

There are several types of internal combustion engines classified as reciprocating or rotary engine; spark ignition or compression ignition engine; and alternative-fuel engine or hybrid-electric engine.

#### Reciprocating Engines

A reciprocating engine consists of (1) compression of air or pre-compressed air (or air-fuel mixture in the case of certain types of engines) within the cylinder of the engine by the action of a piston, (2) addition of heat energy into the compressed air by directly combusting the fuel in the compressed air, followed by (3) expansion of the hot pressurized combustion products in the cylinder against the piston connected to the load to produce useful work. The auto engine and the diesel engine are examples of a reciprocating engine. The compression ratio of an auto engine is lower and the combustion process is initiated by a spark plug while in a diesel engine, the compression ratio is significantly higher and the fuel is ignited by the heat of compression.

#### Spark Ignition Engines

Next, there are two types of spark ignition engines: the four-stroke cycle engine and the two-stroke cycle engine. In the four-stroke engine, four strokes of the piston are required to complete a cycle: (1) intake stroke where the piston moves with the intake valve open and the exhaust valve closed such that a mixture of air with atomized and vaporized fuel is taken into the cylinder, (2) compression stroke, in which the air/fuel mixture is compressed with both valves closed followed by ignition of the air/fuel charge by a timed spark, (3) power or expansion stroke with both valves closed, and finally (4) the exhaust stroke in which the pistons moves with the exhaust valve open and thus completing the cycle. The cylinder walls are cooled by circulating a cooling medium through the cylinder jackets.

In the two-stroke engine, the intake and exhaust strokes are eliminated by using precompressed intake charge to displace the exhaust gases. The two-stroke engine has the advantage of a high power to weight ratio because the engine has a power stroke each revolution. This advantage, however, is offset by the loss of a portion of the intake charge with the exhaust gases, resulting in lower efficiencies. The two-stroke engine has thus limited applications such as in small boat engines, lawnmower engines where low cost and weight are more important than efficiency.

### Compression Ignition Engines

With a sufficiently high compression ratio and a suitable fuel, auto ignition occurs in a reciprocating engine. The engine is similar to the spark ignited engines described above except that during the compression stroke, only air is taken into the piston and compressed to ignition conditions and then, the fuel is atomized directly into the combustion chamber at a controlled rate.

The core of the engine is the cylinder, with the piston moving up and down inside the cylinder. Most cars have more than one cylinder (four, six and eight cylinders are common). In a multi-cylinder engine, the cylinders usually are arranged in one of three ways: inline, V or flat. Different configurations have different advantages and disadvantages in terms of smoothness, manufacturing cost and shape characteristics. These advantages and disadvantages make them more suitable for certain vehicles.

Let's look at some key engine parts in more detail:

### Spark plug

The spark plug supplies the spark that ignites the air/fuel mixture so that combustion can occur. The spark must happen at just the right moment for things to work properly.

### Valves

The intake and exhaust valves open at the proper time to let in air and fuel and to let out exhaust. Note that both valves are closed during compression and combustion so that the combustion chamber is sealed.

### Piston

A piston is a cylindrical piece of metal that moves up and down inside the cylinder.

### Piston Rings

Piston rings provide a sliding seal between the outer edge of the piston and the inner edge of the cylinder. The rings serve two purposes: They prevent the fuel/air mixture and exhaust in the combustion chamber from leaking into the sump during compression and combustion.

They keep oil in the sump from leaking into the combustion area, where it would be burned and lost. Most cars that "burn oil" and have to have a quart added every 1,000 miles are burning it because the engine is old and the rings no longer seal things properly.

## Unit 2　STRUCTURE OF ENGINE

### 阅读材料

**材料1（参考译文）**

#### 发动机的分类

发动机是汽车的心脏，其功能是将燃料转换成能量使汽车行驶。目前，能量转换的最简单方法是让燃料在发动机内部燃烧。因此，汽车发动机是内燃机，即燃料在气缸内燃烧，并将燃烧的膨胀力转换成旋转力用来驱动汽车。

内燃机可分为往复式或旋转式发动机、火花点火式或压燃点火式发动机和替代燃料发动机或混合动力发动机三大类。

**往复式发动机**

往复式发动机的工作过程包括：(1)通过活塞运动来压缩或者预压缩发动机气缸内的空气(或对于某些类型的发动机来说，为空气燃料混合物)；(2)通过直接燃烧压缩空气中的燃料来增加压缩空气的热能；(3)气缸中的高温高压燃烧产物膨胀推动连接在负载上的活塞做有用功。汽车发动机和柴油发动机就是往复式发动机的例子。汽油发动机的压缩比低，燃烧过程是由火花塞点燃的；而柴油发动机的压缩比明显较高，燃料是由压缩生热点燃的。

**火花点火式发动机**

火花点火式发动机有两种类型：四冲程和二冲程。在四冲程发动机中，活塞完成一个周期须经过四个行程：(1)在进气行程中，活塞运动，进气门打开，排气门关闭，这样雾化和蒸发的空气/燃料混合气被吸进气缸；(2)在压缩行程中，进/排气门均关闭，其中空气/燃料混合气被压缩，随后被正时火花点燃；(3)做功或膨胀行程，进/排气门均关闭；(4)排气行程，在此行程中，活塞向下运动，排气门打开，从而完成一个周期。气缸壁通过缸套被循环流动的冷却介质冷却。

【参考图文】

在二冲程发动机中，进气和排气行程被取消，通过使用预压缩进气交换取代排气行程。二冲程发动机具有功重比高的优点，因为发动机的每个循环就有一次做功行程。但是这一优势被进气和排气交换时产生的部分能量损失抵消，结果导致效率较低。二冲程发动机的这些特点，使它的应用被限制在一定领域，如小船的发动机、割草机发动机，其较低的成本和较小的质量比其效率更为重要。

**压燃点火式发动机**

有了足够高的压缩比和合适的燃料，自动点火发生在往复式发动机上。该发动机如上面所述，只是在压缩行程，仅有空气被带到活塞附近并被压缩满足点火条件，然后燃油被雾化以一定的速度直接进入燃烧室。

发动机的核心是气缸，活塞在气缸内做向上和向下运动。大多数汽车有多个气缸(四缸、六缸、八缸是常见的类型)。在多缸发动机上，气缸通常以下面三种方式之一排列：直列、V形或水平。不同的布置方式在工作平稳程度、制造成本和形状特征方面具有不同的优点和缺点。这些优点和缺点使其更适合特定车辆。

下面详细介绍发动机的一些关键部件。

### 火花塞

火花塞提供火花，用来点燃空气/燃油混合气，使其进行燃烧。火花必须在正确的时刻产生才能正常工作。

### 气门

进气门和排气门在适当的时刻打开，让空气和燃料进入气缸，并让废气排出。应注意在压缩和燃烧过程中，这两个气门均被关闭，以保证燃烧室密封。

### 活塞

活塞是一个可以在气缸内向上和向下运动的圆柱形金属块。

### 活塞环

活塞环在活塞外缘与气缸内缘之间形成一个滑动的密封。活塞环有两个目的：在压缩和做功行程中，它们防止燃烧室内的燃料/空气混合气泄漏到油底盘。

它们阻止润滑油进入燃烧区域，从而避免润滑油在燃烧区域燃烧，造成损耗。由于发动机老化和活塞环的密封性能下降，大多数汽车会出现"烧机油"现象，每行驶1000英里被燃烧的机油将增加1quart（夸脱）（美制，1quart＝0.946L；英制，1quart＝1.136L）。

## Passage 2

## How an Engine Works

Since the same process occurs in each cylinder, we will take a look at one cylinder to see how the four-stroke process works. The four strokes are intake, compression, power and exhaust. The piston travels down on the intake stroke, up on the compression stroke, down on the power stroke and up on the exhaust stroke.

### Intake

As the piston starts down on the intake stroke, the intake valve opens and the air-fuel mixture is drawn into the cylinder when the piston reaches the bottom of the intake stroke, the intake valve closes, trapping the air-fuel mixture in the cylinder.

### Compression

The piston moves up and compresses the trapped air-fuel mixture that was brought in by the intake stroke. The amount that the mixture is compressed is determined by the compression ratio of the engine. The compression ratio on the average engine is in the range of 8∶1 to 10∶1.

This means that when the piston reaches the top of the cylinder, the air-fuel mixture is squeezed to about one tenth of its original volume.

# Unit 2  STRUCTURE OF ENGINE

### Power

The spark plug fires, igniting the compressed air-fuel mixture which produces a powerful expansion of the vapor. The combustion process pushes the piston down the cylinder with great force turning the crankshaft to provide the power to propel the vehicle. Each piston fires at a different time, determined by the engine firing order. By the time the crankshaft completes two revolutions, each cylinder in the engine will have gone through one power stroke.

### Exhaust

With the piston at the bottom of the cylinder, the exhaust valve opens to allow the burned exhaust gas to be expelled to the exhaust system. Since the cylinder contains so much pressure, when the valve opens, the gas is expelled with a violent force(that is why a vehicle without a muffler sounds so loud). The piston travels up to the top of the cylinder pushing all the exhaust out before closing the exhaust valve in preparation for starting the four-stroke process over again.

### Oiling System

Oil is the life-blood of the engine. An engine running without oil will last about as long as a human without blood. Oil is pumped under pressure to all the moving parts of the engine by an oil pump. The oil pump is mounted at the bottom of the engine in the oil pan and is connected by a gear to either the crankshaft or the camshaft. This way, when the engine is turning, the oil pump is pumping. There is an oil pressure sensor near the oil pump that monitors pressure and sends this information to a warning light or a gauge on the dashboard. When you turn the ignition key on, but before you start the car, the oil light should light, indicating that there is no oil pressure yet, but also letting you know that the warning system is working. As soon as you start cranking the engine to start it, the light should go out indicating that there is oil pressure.

### Engine Cooling

Internal combustion engines must maintain a stable operating temperature, not too hot and not too cold. With the massive amounts of heat that is generated from the combustion process, if the engine did not have a method for cooling itself, it would quickly self-destruct. Major engine parts can warp causing oil and water leaks and the oil will boil and become useless.

## Engine Balance

### Flywheel

A 4-cylinder engine produces a power stroke every half crankshaft revolution, an 8-cylinder, every quarter revolution. This means that a V8 will be smoother running than a 4. To keep the combustion pulses from generating a vibration, a flywheel is attached to the back of the crankshaft. The flywheel is a disk that is about 12 to 15 inches in diameter.

### Balance Shaft

Some engines have an inherent rocking motion that produces an annoying vibration while running. To combat this, engineers employ one or more balance shafts. A balance shaft is a heavy shaft that runs through the engine parallel to the crankshaft. This shaft has large weights that, while spinning, offset the rocking motion of the engine by creating an opposite rocking motion of their own.

## 材料2（参考译文）

### 发动机如何工作

因为相同的过程发生在每个气缸，所以我们观察一个气缸，就可了解其四个行程的工作过程。四行程是指进气、压缩、做功、排气四个行程。活塞在进气行程下降，压缩行程上升，做功行程下降，排气行程上升。

### 进气行程

活塞在进气行程中开始下降，进气门打开，空气和燃油混合物被吸入气缸。当活塞到达进气行程的底部时，进气门关闭，将空气燃油混合气密封在气缸内。

### 压缩行程

活塞向上移动，压缩在进气行程中吸入的空气燃油混合气。该混合气的压缩量是由发动机压缩比决定的。发动机压缩比的平均范围为8∶1～10∶1。

这意味着，当活塞到达气缸顶部时，空气燃油混合气被压缩到原来的约1/10。

### 做功行程

火花塞点火，点燃被压缩的空气燃油混合气，产生强大的膨胀蒸气。燃烧过程产生很大的作用力推动活塞沿气缸向下运动，带动曲轴开始旋转产生推力使汽车行驶。每个活塞在不同的时间点火，其点火时间由发动机点火顺序决定。此时曲轴转两圈，发动机内的每个气缸经历一次做功行程。

### 排气行程

此时活塞在气缸底部，排气门打开，燃烧过的废气被推入排气系统。由于气缸内压力较大，当阀门打开时，气体将被巨大的压力排出（这就是为什么没有消音器的汽车声音太响）。活塞移动到气缸顶部，在排气门关闭之前排出所有的废气并为重新开始下一个四冲程做准备。

### 润滑系统

润滑油是发动机的血液。发动机无润滑油运行就像人没有血液一样。润滑油在油压作用下通过油泵流到发动机的所有运动部件。油泵被安装在发动机底部的油底壳中，并通过一个齿轮被连接到曲轴或凸轮轴上。这样，当发动机转动时，油泵开始泵油。在油泵的附近装有机油压力传感器,用来监控油泵压力并将这些信息发送到报警灯或仪表板上的测量装置。当打开点火钥匙时,但在起动汽车之前,机油灯应点亮,表示此时没有机油压力,同时也让驾驶员知道报警系统工作正常。一旦起动发动机,报警灯将熄灭表明有机油压力。

**发动机冷却系统**

发动机必须保持一个稳定的工作温度,不太热也不太冷。燃烧过程产生了大量的热量,如果发动机没有一个自身的冷却方法,它会很快自我损坏。发动机的大部分零件会变形从而导致润滑油和冷却液泄漏,进而使润滑油沸腾,变得毫无用处。

## 发动机的平衡

### 飞轮

一个四缸发动机曲轴每转1/2圈飞轮产生一个做功行程,一个八缸发动机曲轴每转1/4圈飞轮产生一个做功行程。这意味着,V8发动机将比四缸发动机运转更平稳。为了防止燃烧脉冲产生振动,飞轮被固定在曲轴后面。飞轮是一个直径为12~15in的圆盘。

### 平衡轴

一些发动机会有内部的摇摆运动,在发动机运行过程中产生令人烦恼的振动。为了解决这个问题,工程师们采用一个或多个平衡轴。平衡轴是一个较重的轴,通过发动机运行与曲轴平行。这个轴重量较大,旋转时通过自身产生的与发动机的摇摆运动方向相反的摇摆运动,抵消发动机的摇摆运动。

# Unit 3

# CRANKSHAFT-CONNECTING ROD MECHANISM
# 曲柄连杆机构

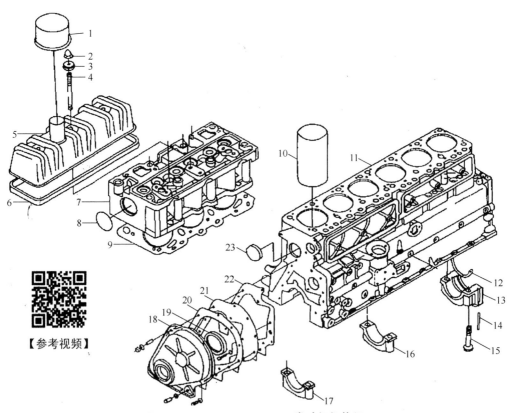

图 3.1 Engine block group 发动机机体组

1—air filter assembly of crankcase 曲轴箱通风空气滤清器总成；2—cover nut 罩盖螺母；3—seal ring 密封圈；4—bolt 螺栓；5—cylinder head cover 气缸盖罩；6—cylinder head cover gasket 气缸盖罩垫片；7—cylinder head 气缸盖；8、23—cup plug 水堵；9—cylinder head gasket 气缸衬垫；10—dry type cylinder jacket 干式气缸套；11—cylinder block 气缸体；12、14—seal 密封条；13、16、17—end, middle, front main bearing lid 后、中间、前主轴承盖；15—main bearing bolt 主轴承螺栓；18—timing gear cap 正时齿轮室盖；19—crankshaft front-end oil seal 曲轴前油封；20、22—liner 衬垫；21—backing plate 垫板

# Unit 3　CRANKSHAFT-CONNECTING ROD MECHANISM

【参考图文】

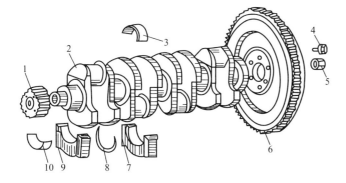

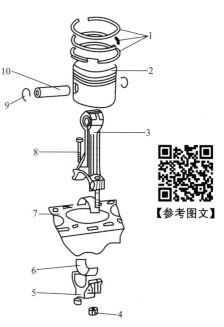

【参考图文】

图 3.2　Composition of crank flywheel group　曲柄飞轮组
1—crankshaft timing pulley 曲柄正时带轮；2—crankshaft 曲轴；
3—upper piece main bearing 上片主轴承；4—flywheel fastening
bolt 飞轮紧固螺栓；5—needle roller bearing 滚针轴承；
6—flywheel 飞轮；7—the second main bearing lid
第二道主轴承盖；8—thrust gasket 止推垫片；
9—the first main bearing lid 第一道主轴承盖；
10—under piece main bearing 下片主轴承

图 3.3　Group of piston and
connecting rod　活塞连杆组
1—piston ring 活塞环；2—piston 活塞；
3—connecting rod 连杆；
4—connecting rod nut 连杆螺母；
5—connecting rod lid 连杆盖；
6—connecting rod bearing 连杆轴承；
7—cylinder block 气缸体；
8—connecting rod bolt 连杆螺栓；
9—piston pin clasp 活塞销卡环；
10—piston pin 活塞销

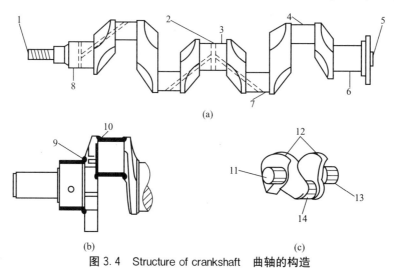

图 3.4　Structure of crankshaft　曲轴的构造
(a) crankshaft 曲轴；(b) the over fillet of journal ends 轴颈两端的过渡圆角；(c) counterweights 平衡重
1—front end axis 前端轴；2—lubricant gallery 润滑油道；3、6、8、11、13—journal 主轴颈；
4、14—crank pin 连杆轴颈；5—crankshaft collar 曲轴后端凸缘；7—crank 曲柄；
9—journal shoulder 主轴颈圆角；10—crank pin shoulder 曲柄销轴；12—counterweights 平衡重

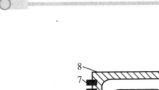
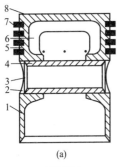

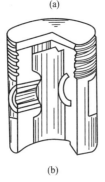
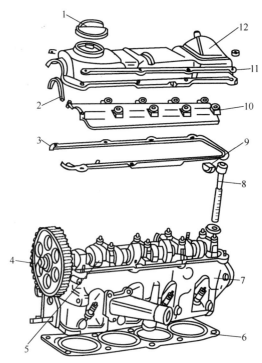

图 3.5　Structure of piston　活塞的构造
（a）full profile 全剖面图；
（b）partial profile 局部剖面图
1—piston skirt 活塞裙部；
2—piston pin clasp 活塞销卡环；
3—piston pin 活塞销；
4—piston pin wall 活塞销座；
5—piston head 活塞头部；
6—stiffening rib 加强筋；
7—piston ring 活塞环；
8—piston crown 活塞顶部

图 3.6　Cylinder cap and gasket　气缸盖和气缸垫
1—fuel filler lid 加油口盖；2—seal 密封条；
3—cylinder head cover sealing gasket 气缸盖罩密封垫；
4—camshaft timing pulley 凸轮轴正时带轮；
5—camshaft 凸轮轴；6—cylinder gasket 气缸垫；
7—cylinder head 气缸盖；
8—cylinder head bolt 气缸盖螺栓；
9—plug 堵头；10—oil guiding slab 导油板；
11—cylinder head cover bead 气缸盖罩压条；
12—cylinder head cover 气缸盖罩

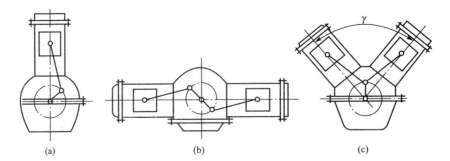

图 3.7　Structure of cylinder body　气缸体的结构形式
（a）inline type 直列式；（b）horizontal type 水平式；（c）V type V 形

## Unit 3  CRANKSHAFT-CONNECTING ROD MECHANISM

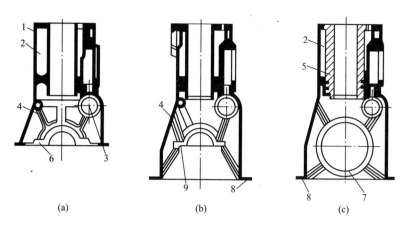

图 3.8  Structure of crankcase  曲轴箱的结构形式

(a)plane-bedded cylinder 平底式气缸；(b)planer type 龙门式；(c)tunnel type 隧道式

1—cylinder block 气缸体；2—cooling jacket 水套；3—camshaft block hole 凸轮轴座孔；
4—stiffening rib 加强筋；5—wet-type cylinder liner 湿缸套；6—main bearing wall 主轴承座；
7—main bearing block hole 主轴承座孔；8—installation of oil pan machining plane 安装油底壳的加工面；
9—installation of main bearing lid machining plane 安装主轴的轴承盖加工面

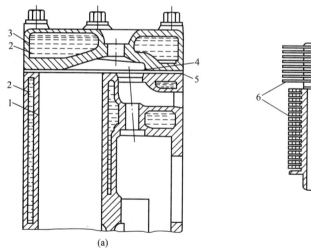 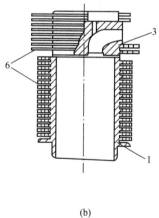

【参考图文】

图 3.9  Cylinder block and head  发动机的气缸体和气缸盖

(a) water jacket of coolant engine 水冷式发动机的水套；
(b) radiator grill of air-cooled engine 风冷式发动机的散热片

1—cylinder block 气缸体；2—cooling water jacket 水套；3—cylinder head 气缸盖；
4—combustion chamber 燃烧室；5—cylinder gasket 气缸垫；6—radiator 散热片

图 3.10　Combustion chamber of gasoline engine
汽油发动机燃烧室

1—hemispheric chamber 半球形；2—multiple spherical 多球形；3—wedge-shape 楔子形；
4—basin shaped 浴盆形；5—pent-roof-shaped 篷形；
6—tundish-shaped 漏斗形

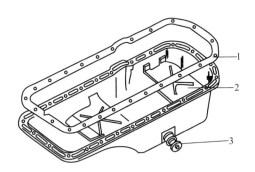

图 3.11　Oil pan　油底盘

1—liner 衬垫；
2—stabilizing oil shield 稳油挡板；
3—magnetic drain plug 磁性放油螺塞

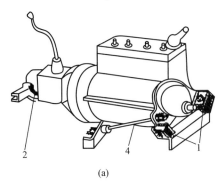

图 3.12　Engine supports　发动机支承

（a）three-points support 三点支承；（b）four-points supports 四点支承

1—front supports 前支承；2—behind supports 后支承；3—rubber skid 橡胶垫块；4—pull rod 拉杆

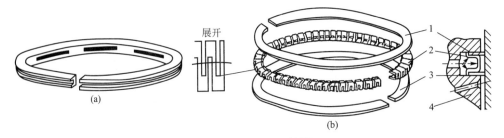

图 3.13　Oil ring　油环

（a）profile 轮廓；（b）structure 结构

1—top segment 上刮片；2—expander 衬簧；3—bottom segment 下刮片；4—piston 活塞

# Unit 3 CRANKSHAFT-CONNECTING ROD MECHANISM

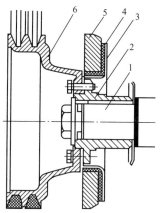

图 3.14 Rubber crankshaft torsional bration damper 橡胶式曲轴扭转减振器

1—front-end crankshaft 曲轴前端；
2—pulley hub 皮带轮轮毂；3—shock absorber disc 减振器盘；4—rubber earing 橡胶垫；5—inertial disc 惯性盘；
6—pulley 带轮

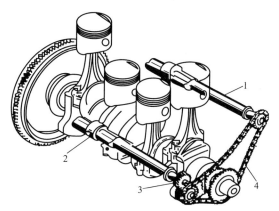

图 3.15 Two balance shafts with four linear cylinders 直列四缸型双平衡轴

1—right balancer shaft and balance weight 右平衡轴及平衡重；
2—left balancer shaft and balance weight 左平衡轴及平衡重；
3—drive gear 传动齿轮；4—driving chain 传动链条

## Reading Materials

### Passage 1

Pistons, Connecting Rods, Crankshafts

#### Pistons

The engine piston is the workhorse of the engine. It is round and made in a variety of sizes to fit the cylinders in the block. Pistons serve several purposes:

(1) Transmit force of expansion to crankshaft through connecting rod.

(2) Act as a guide for upper end of connecting rod.

(3) Serve as a carrier for piston rings used to seal piston in cylinder.

(4) Aid in the burning of the fuel mixture by introducing a swirling action to the air-fuel mixture, which is particularly true in the case of diesel engine pistons. The swirling is accomplished by altering the contour of the piston head.

Pistons operate under exceedingly difficult mechanical and thermal conditions so they must be made and installed with the utmost care. Pistons must be strong enough to stand the force of the expansion, yet light enough to avoid excessive inertia forces when their direction of travel is reversed twice each revolution.

#### Connecting Rods

The connecting rods link the pistons with the crankshaft. In operation, the connecting rod is subjected to both gas pressure and inertia loads, and therefore, it must be adequately strong and rigid and light in weight as well. Connecting rods are generally fabricated from a high-quality steel in the form of a bar with ring shaped heads at its ends. The heads are being known as the connecting rod big end and small end, and serving to attach the rod to the crank pin and the gudgeon pin of the piston respectively.

### Crankshafts

The crankshaft is regarded as the "backbone" of the engine. Connecting rods are attached to the crankshaft. This is where reciprocating engine is converted to rotating energy. The area where the rod connected to the crankshaft is called a journal. They are precisely surfaced to provide smooth operation. For every cylinder in the engine, there will be a journal where the connecting rod connects.

The crankshaft consists of main bearing journals, crank pins, front end, and a rear end. There are usually a series of offset weights to counterbalance the rotation of the crankshaft. The main bearing journals and crank pins are induction hardened to improve their wear resistance. The front of the crankshaft carries a gear or sprocket that drives the camshaft. The fan-belt pulley is also located at the front of the crankshaft along with a heavy balanced disc called a vibration damper. A flywheel is bolted to the rear of the crankshaft. This is a large gear about 20 inches in diameter which the starter will engage to crank the engine for starting.

The crankshaft is located at the bottom side of the cylinder block and is covered by what is called the pan. The area within the pan is called the crankcase. A removable plug is located at the back end of the pan to simplify the removal of oil during an oil change.

 阅读材料

### 材料1（参考译文）

## 活塞、连杆、曲轴

### 活塞

发动机活塞是发动机的主力。它呈圆形，可做成不同的尺寸适应气缸。活塞有以下几个功能：

(1) 通过连杆增大传递到曲轴上的力。

(2) 为连杆的上端起导向作用。

(3) 作为一个载体，用活塞环来密封气缸中的活塞。

(4) 在空气和燃油的混合气上产生一个涡流作用，帮助燃烧燃油混合气，特别是柴油发动机的活塞更是如此。通过改变活塞头轮廓来产生涡流。

活塞在极度复杂的机械和热条件下工作，因此它们的制作和安装必须小心翼翼。考虑到在曲轴的每一周旋转中活塞的运动方向被翻转两次，活塞必须有足够的强度以承受膨胀力，还要质量小以避免过大的惯性。

## Unit 3　CRANKSHAFT-CONNECTING ROD MECHANISM

**连杆**

连杆连接活塞和曲轴。工作时，连杆受到气体压力和惯性负载共同作用，因此，连杆必须足够稳固与结实，同时质量足够轻。连杆一般用高品质的环形钢。连杆的头部称为连杆大端和小端，分别与连杆轴颈和活塞销连接。

**曲轴**

曲轴被视为"发动机的中枢"。连杆连接在曲轴上，通过连杆将往复式发动机的能量转换为旋转能量。连杆连接在曲轴上的区域称为曲轴轴颈，它们经过表面处理以提供平稳的工作环境。对于发动机的每一个气缸，都有一个轴颈用来连接连杆。

曲轴由主轴颈、连杆轴颈、前端和后端组成。通常有一系列的平衡重用来平衡曲轴的旋转运动。主轴承颈和曲轴轴颈经感应淬火硬化，以提高其耐磨性。曲轴前端装有齿轮或链轮用来驱动凸轮轴。风扇带轮安装在曲轴的前面，沿着被称为减振器的较重的平衡盘布置。飞轮被固定在曲轴后方，它是一个直径约 20in 的大齿轮，起动机与它啮合，用来起动发动机。

曲轴安装在气缸体的底部，被油底盘覆盖。油底盘内的区域称为曲轴箱。一个活塞被安装在油底盘的后端，当更换机油时，简化了操作程序。

## Passage 2

### Piston Material

#### Cast Aluminum

Molten aluminum is poured into a mold, the aluminum cools, and hardens. The casting is then machined. Cast aluminum pistons have a crystalline structure which is not as strong as that of a forged piston.

#### Forged Aluminum

A solid slug of aluminum is pressed, very quickly, and with a great deal of force into a die. The resulting forging is then machined to shape. Forged pistons have a grain structure rather than a crystalline structure, this makes them much stronger, and able to take more punishment. For many years forged pistons were used in racing and extreme high performance street engines, but recently have fallen out of favour, because of their relatively heavy weight.

#### Hyper-eutectic(high pressure)Cast Aluminum

A good compromise between forged, and cast pistons, is casting using high pressure. It has relatively light weight, steel expansion bands, and is just about as strong as forged pistons. Hyper-eutectic pistons are very expensive.

## 材料2（参考译文）

### 活 塞 材 料

#### 铸铝

熔化的铝被浇注到模具中，铝水逐渐冷却并且变硬。然后就可以进行铸造加工。铸造铝活塞具有结晶组织，没有锻铝活塞硬。

#### 锻铝

固体铝块在很大的作用力作用下被快速地压缩到模具里，然后锻造加工成形。锻造活塞具有颗粒组织，而不是结晶组织，这使得它们更加结实，并且能够承受更多的作用力。长期以来，锻造活塞被用于赛车和高性能发动机，但因为它们比较重，逐渐受到冷落。

#### 超共晶（高压）铸铝

这种工艺在铸铝活塞和锻铝活塞之间进行良好的折中，采用高压铸造。它质量相对较轻，像钢一样有韧性，又和锻铝活塞一样结实。超共晶活塞价格非常昂贵。

# Unit 4

# VALVE TRAIN
# 配气机构

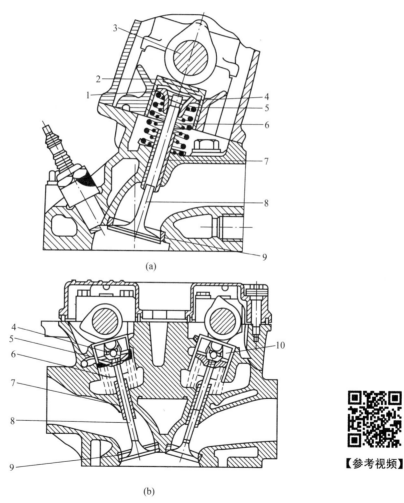

图 4.1 Structure of overhead camshaft and direct drive type valve train
顶置凸轮轴、直接驱动式配气机构
(a) single overhead camshaft 单顶置凸轮轴(SOHC); (b) double overhead camshaft 双顶置凸轮轴(DOHC)
1—mechanical tappet 机械式挺杆; 2—valve clearance adjusting skid 气门间隙调整垫块; 3—camshaft 凸轮轴;
4—valve spring seat 气门弹簧座; 5—valve lock 气门锁片; 6—valve spring 气门弹簧;
7—valve pipe 气门导管; 8—valve 气门; 9—valve seat insert 气门座圈;
10—hydraulic tappet stem 液力挺柱

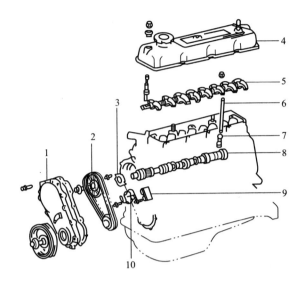

图 4.2　Slide camshaft valve train　侧置凸轮轴式配气机构

1—timing sprocket shield 正时链罩；2—timing chain and sprocket 正时链和链轮；3—camshaft thrust flange 凸轮轴止推凸缘；4—cylinder head cover 气缸盖罩；5—rocker shaft assembly 摇臂轴总成；6—push rod 推杆；7—hydraulic tappet 液压挺杆；8—camshaft 凸轮轴；9—chain shock absorber 链减振器；10—chain tensioning device 链张紧装置

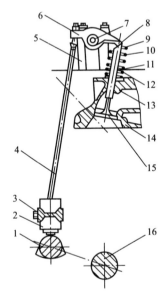

图 4.3　Underhead camshaft valve train　下置凸轮轴式配气机构

1—camshaft 凸轮轴；2—tappet 气门挺杆；3—tappet guide way 挺杆导向体；4—push rod 推杆；
5—rocker bearing block 摇臂轴承座；6—rocker 摇臂；7—rocker shaft 摇臂轴；
8—valve spring place 气门弹簧座；9—valve clearance 气门间隙；
10—valve lock 气门锁片；11—valve oil seal 气门油封；
12—valve spring 气门弹簧；13—valve pipe 气门导管；
14—valve seat 气门座；15—valve 气门；
16—crankshaft 曲轴

# Unit 4　VALVE TRAIN

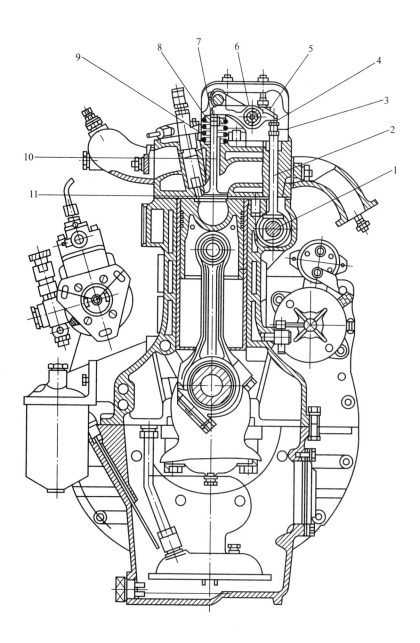

**图 4.4**　Engine with middle camshaft valve train　采用中置凸轮轴式配气机构的发动机

1—camshaft 凸轮轴；2—tappet 挺杆；3—locking nut 锁紧螺母；4—valve clearance adjusting bolt 气门间隙调整螺钉；5—rocker 摇臂；6—rocker shaft 摇臂轴；
7—valve lock 气门锁片；8—valve spring place insert 气门弹簧座；
9—valve spring 气门弹簧；10—valve 气门；
11—valve seat insert 气门座圈

【参考图文】

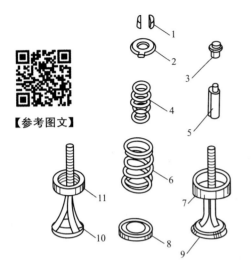

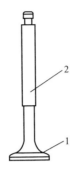

图 4.6　Components of valve 气门的组成
1—head 头部；
2—stem 杆部

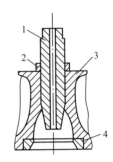

图 4.7　Valve pipe and valve seat 气门导管及气门座
1—valve pipe 气门导管；
2—clasp 卡环；3—cylinder head 气缸盖；4—valve seat 气门座

图 4.5　Parts of valve　气门组零件
1—valve lock 气门锁片；2—valve spring top place 气门弹簧上座；
3—valve oil seal 气门油封；
4—valve internal spring 气门内弹簧；
5—valve pipe 气门导管；6—valve outer spring 气门外弹簧；7—intake valve seat 进气门座；8—valve spring substructure 气门弹簧下座；
9—intake valve 进气门；
10—exhaust valve 排气门；
11—exhaust valve seat 排气门座

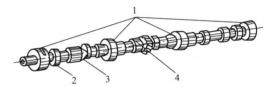

图 4.8　Structure of camshaft 凸轮轴的构造
1—journal 轴颈；2—cam 凸轮；
3—eccentric-cam 偏心轮；
4—sprial gear 螺旋齿轮

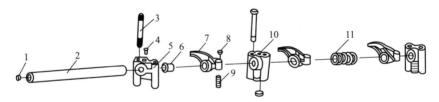

图 4.9　Component of rocker arm assembly 摇臂总成的组成
1—plug 堵头；2—rocker shaft 摇臂轴；3—bolt 螺栓；4—rocker shaft screw 摇臂轴紧固螺钉；
5—rocker shaft bearing 摇臂轴支座；6—rocker bush 摇臂衬套；7—rocker 摇臂；
8—adjusting screw locking nut 调整螺钉锁紧螺母；
9—valve clearance adjusting bolt 气门间隙调整螺钉；
10—rocker shaft middle studdle 摇臂轴中间支撑；
11—location spring 定位弹簧

## Unit 4　VALVE TRAIN

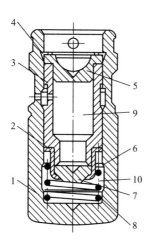

图 4.10　Hydraulic tappet stem　液压挺柱
1—ejector-body 挺柱体；2—one-way valve shelf 单向阀架；3—plunger 柱塞；4—clasp 卡环；5—push rod bearing 推杆支座；6—disc spring 碟形弹簧；7—one-way valve 单向阀；8—plunger spring 柱塞弹簧；9—plunger lumen 柱塞内腔；10—tappet lumen 挺柱体内腔

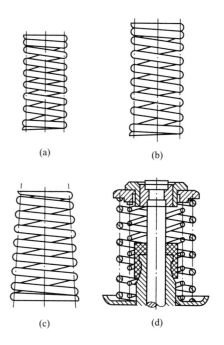

图 4.11　Valve spring　气门弹簧
（a）constant pitch spring 等螺距弹簧；
（b）variable pitch spring 变螺距弹簧；
（c）cone spring 圆锥弹簧；
（d）constant pitch double spring 变螺距双弹簧

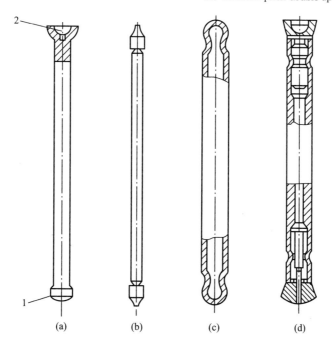

图 4.12　Push rod　推杆
（a）steel solid push rod 钢制实心推杆；（b）duralumin bar push rod 硬铝棒推杆；
（c）、（d）steel pipe push rod 钢制空心推杆
1—spherical ball 球头；2—ball seat 球头座

## Reading Materials

### Passage 1

#### Valve Train

The valves and valve-operating mechanism by which an internal combustion engine takes air or air-fuel mixture into the cylinders and discharges combustion products to the exhaust.

Mechanically, an internal combustion engine is a reciprocating pump, able to draw in a certain amount of air per minute. Since the fuel takes up little space but needs air with which to combine, the power output of an engine is limited by its air-pumping capacity. The flow through the engine should be restricted as little as possible. This is the first requirement for valves. The second is that the valves close off the cylinder firmly during the compression and power strokes.

In most four-stroke engines the valves are the inward-opening poppet type, with the valve head ground to fit a conical seat in the cylinder block or cylinder head. The valve is streamlined and as large as possible to give maximum flow, yet of low inertia so that it follows the prescribed motion at high engine speed.

Engine valves are usually opened by cams that rotate as part of a camshaft, which may be located in the cylinder block or cylinder head. Riding on each cam is a cam follower or valve lifter, which may have a flat or slightly convex surface or a roller, in contact with the cam. The valve is opened by force applied to the end of the valve stem. A valve rotator may be used to rotate the valve slightly as it opens. In engines with the camshaft and valves in the cylinder head, the cam may operate the valve directly through a cup-type cam follower.

阅读材料

**材料1（参考译文）**

### 配气机构

在内燃机上，气门和气门操作机构的功用是将空气和燃油混合气吸入气缸，同时将燃烧的废气排出气缸。

机械上，内燃机是一个往复泵，每分钟能够吸入一定量的空气。由于燃油占用空间小，且需要与空气结合，发动机的输出功率受到吸入空气能力的限制。通过发动机的空气流量应尽可能少地受到限制，这是对气门的第一个要求。第二个要求是在压缩和做功行程中，气门封闭气缸应该牢固可靠。

在大多数四冲程发动机中，气门是内开启型，气门头较平以适应在缸体或缸盖上的锥形气门座。气门结构被简化，尽可能提供最大的流量，具有较小的惯性，使其能够按

## Unit 4　VALVE TRAIN

照发动机在高速运转时的要求工作。

发动机气门通常利用凸轮打开。旋转的凸轮是凸轮轴的一部分，它可以被安装在缸体或缸盖上。每个凸轮推动的是凸轮从动件或气门举升机构，它有一个较平面或较小凸面或一个滚轮。气门通过作用在气门杆末端上的压力被打开。当它打开时，一个旋转阀被用来轻轻地旋转气门。对于凸轮轴和气门安装在气缸盖上的发动机，凸轮可以通过阀杯式凸轮从动件直接控制气门。

### Passage 2

### Valve Springs

Cams, lifters, push rods, and rocker arms are used to open the valves. But how is the valve closed at the right time? Remember, the cam can only push on the other parts of the valve train. It can not push them. A small, coiled, steel valve spring is needed. It pushes on the valve to force it closed. The valve spring fits under the rocker arm and coils around the shaft(valve stem) of the valve. One end of the valve spring pushes up agaist the top surface of the engine. The other end of valve spring pushes agaist the valve. On top of the spring is a small disk-shaped device called a valve spring retainer. A hole in the center of the retainer allows it to fit over the valve stem. The retainer holds the spring in place.

The clearances between the valve stems and the push rods in engines with a bottom arrangement of valves are adjusted as follows:

Holding the push rod by its flats, ease off lock nut and adjust the clearance with the adjusting screw. Then, holding the adjusting screw and push rod, tighten the lock nut and recheck the clearance. The clearance of the intake/exhaust valves should be adjusted to the required ranges.

The timing chain/belt should be checked during the time that the front main bearing is removed for inspection. Any excessive slack in the chain/belt calls for replacement. When the timing mechanism is to be disassembled, be sure to order a new timing case cover gasket and a front oil seal.

### 材料 2（参考译文）

### 气 门 弹 簧

凸轮、升降器、推杆和摇臂是用来打开气门的。那么如何在正确的时间关闭阀门？需要注意的是，凸轮只能推动气门的一部分，它不能拉动气门。一个较小的、卷曲的、钢质的气门弹簧是必需的。它推动气门，迫使它关闭。气门弹簧安装在摇臂下面，卷曲在气门轴（阀杆）上。气门弹簧的一端推动发动机的顶部，另一端推动气门。弹簧的顶部是一个小圆盘形装置，称为气门弹簧挡圈。挡圈中心有一个孔与阀杆匹配，使阀杆在合适位置。挡圈将弹簧保持在合适的位置。

气门杆与推杆之间的间隙通过安装在发动机上的底部调整阀来调整，方法如下：

保持推杆平稳，放松锁紧螺母，用调节螺钉来调整间隙。接着，保持调整螺钉和推杆不动，拧紧锁紧螺母，重新检查间隙。进、排气门的间隙需要按要求调整到所需的范围。

当前主轴承被取下来检查时，同时需要检查正时链条/传动带。正时链条/传动带链中如有过度松弛时要求更换。当正时机构需要拆卸时，一定要安装一个新的正时齿轮箱密封垫片和一个前端油封。

# Unit 5

# FUEL SUPPLY SYSTEM FOR GASOLINE ENGINE
# 汽油发动机燃油供给系统

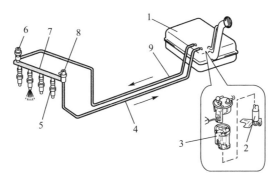

图 5.1  Fuel supply system for gasoline engine  汽油发动机燃油供给系统
1—fuel tank 燃油箱；2—electric fuel pump 电动汽油泵；3—fuel filter 燃油滤清器；
4—rail return pipe 回油管；5—injector 喷油器；6—pulsation damper 脉动阻尼器；
7—distribution pipe 分配油管；8—fuel pressure regulator 油压调节器；
9—oil pipeline 输油管

【参考视频】

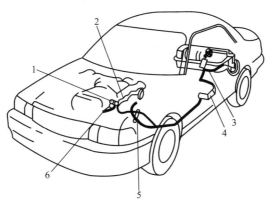

图 5.2  Fuel supply system  燃油供给系统
1—fuel pressure regulator 燃油压力调节器；2—distribution pipe 燃油分配管；
3—electric fuel pump 电动燃油泵；4—fuel filter 燃油滤清器；
5—pulsating damper 脉动阻尼器；6—injector 喷油器

【参考图文】

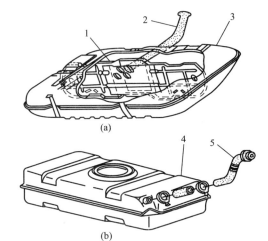

图 5.3　Fuel tank　燃油箱

（a）partial profile 局部剖面图；（b）structure 结构

1—baffle plate 隔板；2、5—fuel delivery tube 加油管；3—fuel tank for passenger car 乘用车油箱；4—fuel tank for wagon 货车油箱

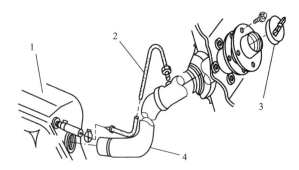

图 5.4　Fuel delivery tube and vent pipe　加油管和通气管

1—fuel tank 油箱；2—vent pipe 通气管；3—tank cap 油箱盖；4—fuel delivery tube 加油管

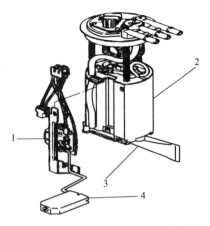

图 5.5　Electric fuel pump and fuel level sensor　电动汽油泵和油面传感器

1—fuel level sensor 油面传感器；2—electric fuel pump 电动汽油泵；
3—fuel filter net 滤网；4—float 浮子

# Unit 5　FUEL SUPPLY SYSTEM FOR GASOLINE ENGINE

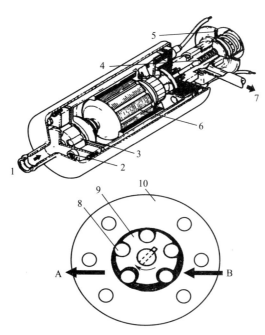

图 5.6　Ball electric fuel pump　滚柱式电动汽油泵

1—fuel inlet 进油口；2—relief valve 限压阀；3—oil pump 油泵；4—check valve 单向阀；
5—buffer 缓冲器；6—electric engine 电动机；7—fuel outlet 出油口；
8—ball 滚柱；9—rotor 转子；10—pump housing 泵体

A—outlet 出油；B—inlet 进油

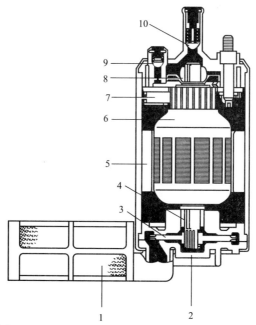

图 5.7　Impeller electric fuel pump　叶轮式电动汽油泵

1—filter net 滤网；2—rubber cushion 橡胶缓冲垫；3—rotor 转子；4—bearing 轴承；
5—magnet 磁铁；6—armature 电枢；7—carbon brush 电刷；8—bearing 轴承；
9—relief net 限压网；10—one-way valve 单向阀

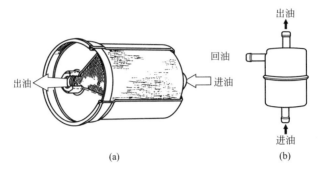

图 5.8　Fuel filter　燃油滤清器

(a) partial profile 局部剖面图；(b) structure 结构

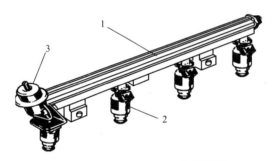

图 5.9　Distribution rail　分配油管

1—distribution rail 分配油管；2—injector 喷油器；
3—fuel pressure regulator 油压调节器

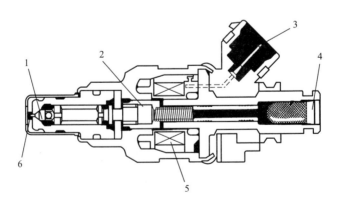

图 5.10　Injector　喷油器

1—needle 针阀；2—armature 电枢；3—plug 插头；4—fuel inlet 进油口；
5—solenoid coil 电磁线圈；6—spray orifice 喷孔

## Unit 5　FUEL SUPPLY SYSTEM FOR GASOLINE ENGINE

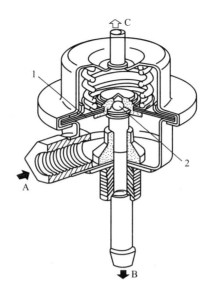

图 5.11　Fuel pressure regulator　油压调节器

1—diaphragm 膜片；2—return valve 回油阀；
A—inlet 进油口；B—outlet 出油口；C—vacuum joint 真空接口

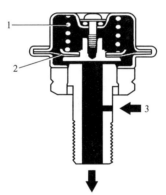

图 5.12　Fuel pressure damper　油压缓冲器

1—spring 弹簧；2—diaphragm 膜片；3—fuel 燃油

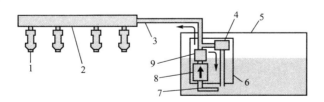

图 5.13　Returnless fuel system　无回油管的燃油系统

1—injector 喷油器；2—distribution pipe 分配油管；3—outlet pipe 输油管；
4—pressure regulator 油压调节器；5—fuel tank 燃油箱；
6—fuel pump and fuel filter assembly 燃油泵及燃油滤清器总成；
7—inlet filter net 进油滤网；8—electric fuel pump 电动汽油泵；
9—fuel filter 燃油滤清器

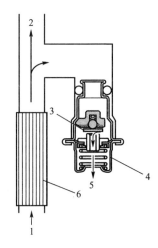

图 5.14　In-tank fuel pressure regulator　燃油箱内的油压调节器

1—inlet filter net 进油滤网；2—outlet pipe 输油管；3—valve 阀；4—fuel pressure regulator 油压调节器；5—return fuel 回油；6—fuel filter 燃油滤清器

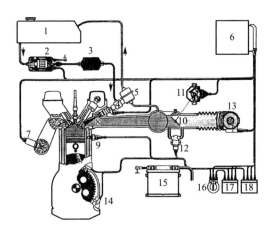

图 5.15　Electric control system for engine　发动机电控系统

1—oil tank 汽油箱；2—electric fuel pump 电动汽油泵；3—fuel filter 燃油滤清器；4—distribution pipe 分配油管；5—fuel pressure regulator 油压调节器；6—ECU 电控单元；7—oxygen sensor 氧传感器；8—injector 喷油器；9—coolant-temperature sensor 冷却液温度传感器；10—throttle 节气门；11—throttle position sensor 节气门位置传感器；12—idle control valve 怠速控制阀；13—flow meter 空气流量计；14—crankshaft position sensor 曲轴位置传感器；15—battery 蓄电池；16—ignition switch 点火开关；17、18—replay 继电器

## Reading Materials

### Passage 1

#### Fuel Supply System for Gasoline Engine—The Basics

The fuel supply system of the vehicle constitutes an important element of an engine.

# Unit 5  FUEL SUPPLY SYSTEM FOR GASOLINE ENGINE

Its core function is to ensure the smooth and uninterrupted supply of fuel to other peripherals of an engine. An automobile fuel supply system comprises of various components and devices like fuel cells, carburetor, fuel pump, fuel tank, fuel coolers, automobile filters which are used for storing fuel and distributing it to internal combustion engine as in when needed. Today, almost every automobile has a pressurized fuel supply system equipped with a pump that is used for pushing fuel from the fuel tank to engine of the vehicle.

An automobile fuel supply system comprises a number of automotive components that assist in supplying fuel to the engine's combustion chamber and regulating it, thereby preventing any loss of fuel.

The fuel supply system for internal combustion engines typically comprise a fuel delivery pipe to which fuel injectors are mounted through connectors, which lead to a fuel tank through a fuel pipe. Further, the connectors of the injectors extend upward to open at an upper portion in the delivery pipe. When the vehicle starts and the air and fuel vapor is produced in the fuel supply system, it is gradually introduced into the delivery pipe and rapidly injected through the connectors and the injectors into the combustion chamber of an engine.

The fuel supply system of an automobile comes into play when the person driving the automobile steps on the gas. The gas pedal is linked to a throttle valve which opens and closes depending upon how much the gas pedal has been pressed. The harder the press, the more fuel supplied to the engine.

All of this is accomplished with the help of a valve called the fuel injector. The injector is capable of opening and closing many times each second as well as atomizing the fuel when it sprays the fuel into the combustion chamber.

### Automobile Filters

An automobile filter or an air filter is a device which purifies the air supplied to the engine by removing dust and other particulates from it. Air filters are essential because the air supplied to an engine needs to be free of pollutants, lest it damages the engine, contaminates the oil or causes it to malfunction. Most of today's automobiles using fuel injection technology utilize a pleated paper filter element in the form of a flat panel. The filter is positioned inside a plastic box linked to the throttle body.

### Carburetor

The carburetor is an automotive component that mixes air and fuel for an internal combustion engine. Invented by Karl Benz before 1885, it's colloquially known as carb in North America and the UK. The construction of a typical carburetor entails a "barrel" through which the air rushes into the inlet manifold of the engine. The shape of the barrel causes the airflow to increase in speed at the narrowest part. Fuel is introduced into the air stream through small holes located at narrowest part of the barrel. This operation mixes air and fuel before it reaches the cylinder through the fuel injector.

### Fuel Cell

Fuel cells are electrochemical conversion devices, which produce electricity from fuel and an oxidant, when they react in the presence of an electrolyte. These cells continue to produce electricity as long as the reactants flow into the cell and the by-products flow out of it. Fuel cells can continue operation continuously till the necessary flows of electrolytes and reactants are maintained.

### Fuel Injection System

Fuel injection system refers to the set of automotive part which mix fuel with air in an internal combustion engine. The primary component of this system is the fuel injector, which is a computer controlled valve. When pressurized fuel is supplied to it, it delivers fine droplets of fuel and air mixture into the combustion chamber of the engine.

It's a sophisticated piece of machinery and can open and close multiple times within a second. The quantity of the fuel supplied to the engine is determined by amount of time the fuel injector stays open. This function is electronically controlled. The system also makes use of a lot of sensors to ensure that the right amount of fuel is sprayed into the cylinders.

### Fuel Pump

The fuel pump is a vacuum device controlled mechanically or electrically to draw gasoline from the tank and supply it to the carburetor or the fuel injector. A fuel pump is an essential component of automobiles. Carburetor and fuel injected engines make use of different kinds of fuel pumps. While carbureted engines utilize low pressure mechanical pumps mounted outside the fuel tank, the fuel injected engines use electric fuel pumps that are mounted inside the fuel tank.

### Fuel Tank

The fuel tank is that part of an automobile engine, which stores the fuel supplied into the engine. Depending upon the type of automobile and fuels, fuel tanks vary in sizes, types and complexity of designs.

 阅读材料

## 材料1（参考译文）

### 汽油发动机燃油供给系统的基础知识

汽车燃油供给系统是构成发动机的一个重要元素。其核心功能是确保给发动机的其他外围设备平稳地，不间断地供应燃油。汽车燃油供给系统由不同的组件和装置组成，

## Unit 5　FUEL SUPPLY SYSTEM FOR GASOLINE ENGINE

如燃料电池装置、化油器、燃油泵、油箱、燃油冷却器、燃油滤清器。它们用来储存燃油并且将燃油适时输送到内燃机中。如今，几乎每个汽车都有一个带油泵的增压燃油供应系统，油泵主要用来将燃油从油箱推进汽车的发动机。

汽车燃油供给系统包括许多汽车零部件，它们协助将燃油供应到发动机的燃烧室，并且调节其压力，从而阻止燃油损失。

一个发动机的燃油供给系统通常包括一个喷油器，它通过连接器被安装在燃油输送管上，连接器通过油管安装在燃油箱上。此外，带有连接器的喷油器向上延伸在输油管上部打开。当汽车起动时，在燃油供给系统中产生空气和燃料蒸气，缓慢进入输油管，同时通过连接器和喷油器迅速喷射到发动机的燃烧室。

当驾驶员驾驶汽车踩加速踏板时，汽车燃油供给系统开始工作，踏板被连接到节气门上，节气门的开启和关闭取决于加速踏板被踩下的程度，被踩下程度越大，越多的燃油被供应到发动机中。

所有这一切工作是在一个被称为喷油器的阀门协助下完成的。喷油器能够每秒钟开闭多次，当它将燃油喷射到燃烧室时可将燃油雾化。

### 汽车滤清器

汽车滤清器或空气滤清器是一种通过除去灰尘和微粒来净化被供应到发动机中空气的装置。空气滤清器是必要的，通过它来确保供应给发动机的空气没有污染物，以免损害发动机、污染润滑油，导致发生故障。当今的汽车大多采用燃油喷射技术，均采用一个平面褶型纸质滤清器。该过滤器被安装在一个塑料盒子内，与节气门体相连接。

### 化油器

对于内燃机来说，化油器是一个用来混合空气和燃料的汽车零部件。在1885年之前，被卡尔·奔驰发明，在北美和英国它被通俗地称为"carb（汽化器）"。典型的化油器结构需要一个"桶"，空气通过它进入发动机的进气歧管。该桶在最窄部分的形状会导致气流速度增加。燃料通过位于该桶最窄部分的小孔被引入到气流中。在到达气缸之前，利用燃油喷射器将空气和燃料混合。

### 燃料电池

燃料电池是一种电化学转换装置，当它们在电解质中发生反应时从燃油和氧化剂中产生电能。只要反应物进入电池的同时反应副产物流出电池，这些电池就能持续产生电能。只要电解质和必要的反应物运作不断得以维持，燃料电池就可以持续工作。

### 燃油喷射系统

燃油喷射系统是汽车的一部分，它将空气与燃油在内燃机内混合。该系统的主要组成部分是燃油喷射器，它是一个计算机控制的阀门。当高压油供应给它时，它将优质的燃油和空气混合气油滴输送到发动机的燃烧室。燃油喷射系统是一个复杂的机械件，可以在一秒钟内打开和关闭多次。供应给发动机油量的多少取决于燃油喷射器保持打开状态的时间长短，该功能由电子控制。该系统还使用了大量的传感器，以确保适量的燃油被喷入气缸。

**燃油泵**

燃油泵是一个通过机械或电子控制的真空设备,用来将汽油从油箱吸出,供应给化油器或燃油喷射器。燃油泵是汽车的重要组成部分。化油器式和燃油喷射式发动机使用不同类型的燃油泵。化油器式发动机采用安装在油箱外面的低压机械式泵,而燃油喷射式发动机使用安装在油箱内的电动燃油泵。

**油箱**

油箱是汽车发动机的一个部分,用来存储供应到发动机的燃油。根据汽车和燃油的种类不同,油箱在大小、类型和设计的复杂性方面有所不同。

Passage 2

## Industry Overview

The growth of the automobile fuel supply system industry is directly linked to the growth of the automobile industry as a whole. While at present the auto industry is going through a downturn in North America and Europe, other markets such as China and Russia are amongst the emerging markets.

Plastics have been replacing steel as the material for the manufacture of fuel tanks. Estimates conclude that about 348,000 tones of steel were lost in 2006 and by 2013 about 419,000 tones of steel could be lost to plastic. The trend is expected to continue till the market is saturated. The increasing popularity of plastics is attributed to their being noncorrosive, lighter and more flexible than metal.

On another front the market potential for fuel-injection systems is also looking up owing to increasing environmental concerns. In fact, reduction in exhaust emissions has already been witnessed due to the improvements in diesel engine design in Europe. The newer designs while lead to decrease emission, enhance the automobile engine's performance.

Furthermore, technologies such as hybrid and electric cars are fast becoming popular around the world, which also require different fuel-injection systems. Also, fuel cells are expected to power these vehicles. On the whole the outlook for automobile fuel supply systems is promising.

**材料 2(参考译文)**

### 行 业 概 况

汽车燃料供给系统行业的增长,直接关系到作为一体的汽车产业的增长。虽然目前汽车行业在北美和欧洲的市场持续低迷,但其他地区,如中国和俄罗斯,已经成为新兴市场。

塑料已经取代钢材作为燃油箱的制造材料。2006年约有34.8万t的钢材被塑料所取代,预计到2013年将约41.9万t的钢材会被塑料取代。这种趋势预计将持续到市场饱

## Unit 5  FUEL SUPPLY SYSTEM FOR GASOLINE ENGINE

和。由于塑料具有耐腐蚀性、比金属更轻、更灵活，它的应用日益普及。

另外，对环境问题的日益关注，也增加了燃油喷射系统的市场潜力。实际上，在欧洲人们已经目睹了通过改进柴油发动机设计来减少废气排放的事实。新设计将使排放减少，提高汽车发动机的性能。

此外，新技术如混合动力和电动汽车迅速在世界各地普及，也需要不同的燃油喷射系统。同时，燃料电池可能成为这些新技术车辆的动力。整体来讲，汽车燃料供给系统的前景是广阔的。

# Unit 6

# GASOLINE ENGINE IGNITION SYSTEM
# 汽油发动机点火系统

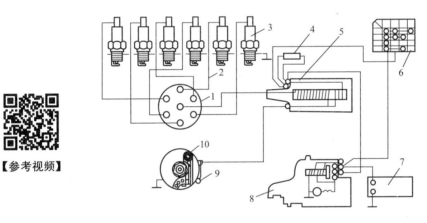

图 6.1　Conventional ignition system　传统点火系统

1—ignition distributor 点火分电器；2—ignition cable 高压导线；3—spark plug 火花塞；4—ballast resistor 附加电阻；5—ignition coil 点火线圈；6—ignition switch 点火开关；7—battery 蓄电池；
8—starter 起动机；9—capacitor 电容器；10—breaker 断电器

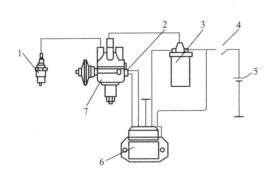

图 6.2　Electronic ignition system　电子点火系统

1—spark plug 火花塞；2—ignition signal generator 点火信号发生器；3—ignition coil 点火线圈；
4—ignition switch 点火开关；5—battery 蓄电池；6—electronic igniter 电子点火器；
7—distributor assembly 分电器总成

# Unit 6　GASOLINE ENGINE IGNITION SYSTEM

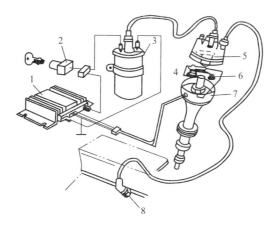

图 6.3　Photoelectric electronic ignition system　光电式电子点火系统

1—igniter 点火器；2—ignition switch 点火开关；3—ignition coil 点火线圈；4—photoelectric ignition signal generator 光电式点火信号发生器；5—rotor 转子，分火头；6—shade chassis 遮光盘；7—ignition distributor 分电器；8—spark plug 火花塞

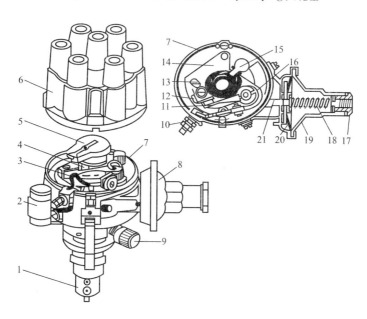

图 6.4　Structure of distributor　分电器

1—coupling 万向节；2—capacitor 电容器；3—contact and breaker plate 触点及断电器底板组成；4—cam 凸轮；5—rotor 转子，分火头；6—distributor cap 分电器盖；7—distributor shell 分电器壳体；8—vacuum advance regulator 真空提前调节器；9—oil cup 油杯；10—connector 接线柱；11—active point leg 活动触点臂；12—contact 触点；13—eccentric screw 偏心螺钉；14—active plate 活动底板；15—oil felt and clamp ring 油毡及夹圈；16—contact spring piece 触点臂弹簧片；17—nut 螺母；18—spring 弹簧；19—vacuum advance regulator package 真空提前调节器外壳；20—vacuum advance regulator diaphragm 真空提前调节器膜片；21—connecting rod 拉杆

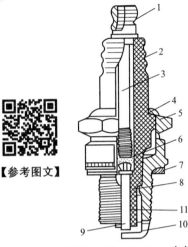

图 6.5　Spark plug　火花塞

1—connecting nut 接线螺母；2—insulator 绝缘体；
3—metal rod 金属杆；4—inner gasket 内垫圈；
5—shell 壳体；6—conductor glass 导体玻璃；
7—sealing washer 密封垫圈；8—copper
washer 纯铜垫圈；9—center electrode
中心电极；10—side electrode 侧电极；
11—insulator part 绝缘体裙部

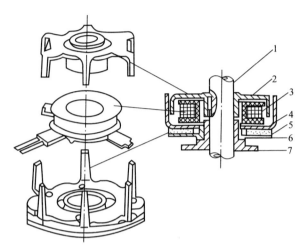

图 6.6　Magnetic pulse type ignition signal generator
磁脉冲式点火信号发生器

1—roter axis 转子轴；2—signal rotor 信号转子；
3—sensor ring 传感器线圈；4—stator 定子；
5—plastic permanent magnetic plate 塑性
永磁片；6—concentrating flux plate
导磁板；7—bottom plate 底板

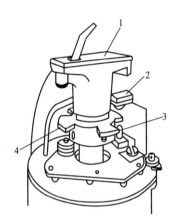

图 6.7　Photoelectric ignition signal generator
光电式点火信号发生器

1—rotor 转子，分火头；2—light source 光源；
3—light receiver 光接收器；
4—shade plate 遮光盘

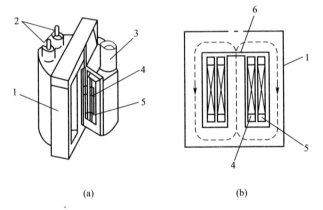

图 6.8　Closed magnetic circuit ignition coil
闭磁路点火线圈

（a）structure 结构；（b）magnetic circuit 磁路
1—"date" glyph iron core "日"字形铁心；2—primary
winding connector 初级线圈接线柱；3—high-voltage
connector 高压接线柱；4—primary winding
初级线圈；5—secondary winding 次级线圈；
6—air clearance 空气间隙

# Unit 6  GASOLINE ENGINE IGNITION SYSTEM

Reading Materials

Passage 1

### Introduction of Ignition System

There are many different types of ignition systems. Most of these systems can be placed into one of three distinct groups: the conventional breaker point type ignition systems(in use since the early 1900s); the electronic ignition systems(popular since the mid 70s); and the distributor less ignition system(introduced in the mid 80s).

The automotive ignition system has two basic functions: it must control the spark and timing of the spark plug firing to match varying engine requirements, and it must increase battery voltage to a point where it will overcome the resistance offered by the spark plug gap and fire the plug. The first step of understanding a vehicle's ignition system is to learn about basic electricity.

### Point-type Ignition System

An automotive ignition system is divided into two electrical circuits——the primary and secondary circuits. The primary circuit carries low voltage. This circuit operates only on battery current and is controlled by the breaker points and the ignition switch. The secondary circuit consists of the secondary windings in the coil, the high tension lead between the distributor and the coil (commonly called the coil wire) on external coil distributors, the distributor cap, the distributor rotor, the spark plug leads and the spark plugs.

The distributor is the controlling element of the system. It switches the primary current on and off and distributes the current to the proper spark plug each time a spark is needed. The distributor is a stationary housing surrounding a rotating shaft. The shaft is driven at one-half engine speed by the engine's camshaft through the distributor drive gears. A cam near the top of the distributor shaft has one lobe for each cylinder of the engine. The cam operates the contact points, which are mounted on a plate within the distributor housing.

A rotor is attached to the top of the distributor shaft. When the distributor cap is in place, a spring-loaded piece of metal in the center of the cap makes contact with a metal strip on top of the rotor. The outer end of the rotor passes very close to the contacts connected to the spark plug leads around the outside of the distributor cap.

The coil is the heart of the ignition system. Essentially, it is nothing more than a transformer which takes the relatively low voltage(12 volts) available from the battery and increases it to a point where it will fire the spark plug as much as 40,000 volts. The term "coil" is perhaps a misnomer since there are actually two coils of wire wound about an iron core. These coils are insulated from each other and the whole assembly is enclosed in an oil-filled case. The primary coil, which consists of relatively few turns of heavy wire, is connected to the two primary terminals located on top of the coil. The secondary coil consists of many turns of fine wire. It is connected to the high-tension connection on top of the coil.

阅读材料

材料1（参考译文）

## 点火系统介绍

点火系统有许多不同的类型。这些系统大部分可以分为三种：传统的断电器式点火系统（在20世纪初使用）、电子点火系统（20世纪70年代中期以来流行）和无分电器式点火系统（出现于20世纪80年代中期）。

汽车点火系统有两个基本功能，它必须控制火花的强度和火花塞的点火时刻以适应发动机的不同需要，而且必须增强蓄电池电压，使它能够克服火花塞的间隙和火花塞所带来的阻力。了解一辆车的点火系统的第一步是要学习基础电学。

### 触点式点火系统

汽车的点火系统分为两个电路——初级电路和次级电路。初级电路产生低电压。该电路仅在蓄电池有电流时工作，受断电器和点火开关控制。次级电路由点火线圈内的次级线圈、在分电器和外部分电器点火线圈（通常被称为主高压线）之间的高张力导线、分电器盖、分火头、火花塞导线和火花塞组成。

分电器是系统的控制部分。它控制初级电流的闭合和打开，并将电流分配到合适的火花塞上以备每一次点火需要。分电器是一个固定在旋转轴周围的壳体，旋转轴通过分电器驱动齿轮被凸轮轴驱动，以发动机一半的速度旋转。在分电器轴顶部有一个凸轮，凸轮上有一个叶片对应发动机的每个气缸。凸轮控制的连接点固定在分电器壳内的一个圆盘上。

转子安装在分电器的顶端。当分电器盖合上时，位于分电器盖中心的一个金属弹簧片与分火头顶部的一个金属片接触。转子的外端紧密连接在分电器盖外端的火花塞导线上。

点火线圈是点火系统的核心。从本质上讲，它只不过是一个变压器，接收由蓄电池提供的较低电压（12V）并将它增强到使火花塞点火的高达40 000V的电压。术语"线圈"，或许是用词不当，因为其实是一个铁心上缠有两个线圈，这些线圈之间相互隔绝且整个装置被密封在充满油的盒子中。初级线圈由圈数相对较少的粗线组成，连接到固定在线圈顶部的两个初级端子上。次级线圈由圈数较多的细线组成，连接到线圈顶部的高压端子上。

Passage 2

## Electronic Ignition Systems

The need for higher mileage, reduced emissions and greater reliability has led to the development of the electronic ignition systems. These systems generate a much stronger

## Unit 6  GASOLINE ENGINE IGNITION SYSTEM

spark which is needed to ignite leaner fuel mixtures. Breaker point systems needed a resistor to reduce the operating voltage of the primary circuit in order to prolong the life of the points. The primary circuits of the electronic ignition systems operate on full battery voltage which helps to develop a stronger spark. Spark plug gaps have widened due to the ability of the increased voltage to jump the larger gap. Cleaner combustion and less deposits have led to longer spark plug life.

On some systems, the ignition coil has been moved inside the distributor cap. This system is said to have an internal coil as opposed to the conventional external one.

Electronic ignition systems are not as complicated as they may first appear. In fact, they differ only slightly from conventional point ignition systems. Like conventional ignition systems, electronic systems have two circuits: a primary circuit and a secondary circuit. The entire secondary circuit is the same as in a conventional ignition system. In addition, the section of the primary circuit from the battery to the terminal at the coil is the same as in a conventional ignition system.

Electronic ignition systems differ from conventional ignition systems in the distributor component area. Instead of a distributor cam, breaker plate, points, and condenser, an electronic ignition system has an armature, a pickup coil, and an electronic control module.

Essentially, all electronic ignition systems operate in the following manner: with the ignition switch turned on, primary (battery) current flows from the battery through the ignition switch to the coil primary windings. Primary current is turned on and off by the action of the armature. As each tooth of the armature nears the pickup coil, it creates a voltage that signals the electronic module to turn off the coil primary current. A timing circuit in the module will turn the current on again after the coil field has collapsed. When the current is off, however, the magnetic field built up in the coil is allowed to collapse, which causes a high voltage in the secondary windings of the coil. It is now operating on the secondary ignition circuit, which is the same as in a conventional ignition system.

## 材料2（参考译文）

### 电子点火系统

为了满足更高的行驶里程需求、减少排放和更高可靠性的需要，催生了电子点火系统的发展。当少量的燃油混合气需要被点燃时，这些系统能够产生较强的火花。断电器式点火系统需要一个电阻，以减少初级电路的工作电压，从而延长该系统的使用寿命。电子点火系统的初级电路在蓄电池电压下工作，有助于产生更强的火花。火花在跳跃较大的间隙时，火花塞的间隙变宽，能够起到增强电压的作用。燃烧越清洁，沉积物越少，火花塞的使用寿命越长。

在某些系统上，点火线圈已经被移至分电器盖内。该系统被认为有一个内部线圈，

49

而不是传统的外部线圈。

电子点火系统首次出现时并不复杂，只是与传统的点火系统略有不同。像传统的点火系统一样，电子系统有两个电路：初级电路和次级电路。整个次级电路与传统点火系统的相同，并且，在初级电路中从蓄电池到线圈的终端部分也与传统的点火系统的相同。

电子点火系统不同于传统的点火系统的地方在于分电器的组成。电子点火系统用一个电枢、一个线圈和一个电子控制模块代替了分电器凸轮、断电器配电盘、开关和电容器。

从本质上讲，所有的电子点火系统都是按照如下方式运作：随着点火开关打开，初级电流（电池）从蓄电池通过点火开关流到初级线圈。初级电流的接通和断开由电枢控制。当电枢上每个齿接近线圈时，它产生一个电压信号输送到电子模块用来断开初级电流；在线圈磁场消失时，模块中的定时电路将再次接通电流。随着电流被断开，线圈中产生的磁场将消失，从而使线圈的次级线圈产生高电压。此时次级点火电路的运行与传统的点火系统相同。

# Unit 7

# GASOLINE ENGINE COMPUTER-AIDED CONTROL SYSTEM
# 汽油发动机计算机辅助控制系统

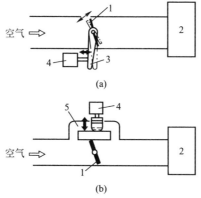

【参考视频】

图 7.1 Air input ways with control idling working conditions 控制怠速工况下进气量的方法
(a) throttle in-line way 节气门直动式；(b) by-pass air way 旁通空气道
1—throttle valve 节气门；2—intake pipe 进气管；3—throttle valve control arm 节气门操纵臂；
4—execution components 执行元件；5—idle air path 怠速空气道

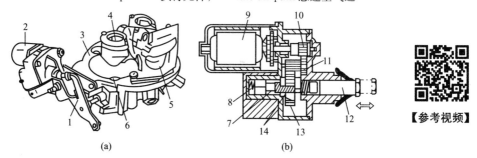

【参考视频】

图 7.2 In-line way throttle idle speed regulator 节气门直动式怠速调节器
(a) outline 外形图；(b) structure 结构图
1—throttle control arm 节气门操纵臂；2—idling controller 怠速控制器；3—throttle body 节气门体；
4—fuel injector 喷油器；5—fuel pressure regulator 油压调节器；6—throttle 节气门；
7—anti-rotating hexagonal hole 防转六角孔；8—springs 弹簧；9—direct current
electromotor 直流电动机；10、11、13—gear 齿轮；12—transmission
shaft 传动轴；14—lead screw 导螺杆

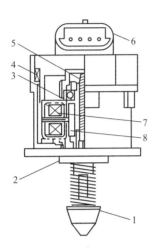

图 7.3 The idle speed control valve of step motor
步进电动机型怠速控制阀

1—control valve 控制阀；2—front-end bearing 前轴承；
3—rear-end bearing 后轴承；4—seal ring 密封圈；
5—lead screw mechanism 丝杠机构；
6—harness connector 线束插接器；
7—stator 定子；8—rotor 转子

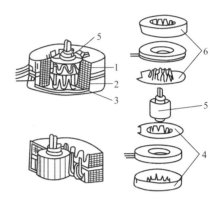

图 7.4 The structure of step motor
步进电动机的结构图

1、2—coil 线圈；3—generator pole 爪极；
4、6—stator 定子；5—rotor 转子

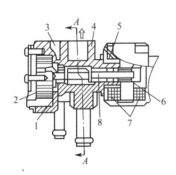

图 7.5 The idle speed controller of rotary solenoid valve
旋转电磁阀型怠速控制阀

1—control valve 控制阀；2—double-metal plate
双金属片；3—cooling fluid chamber 冷却液腔；
4—valve body 阀体；5、7—coil 线圈；
6—permanent magnet 永久磁铁；
8—valve shaft 阀轴

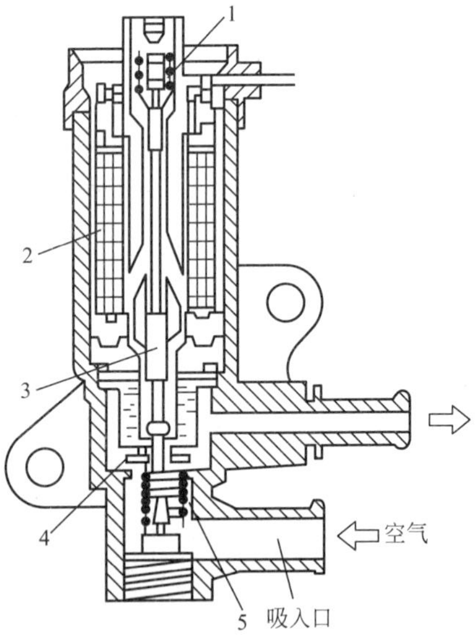

图 7.6 The idle speed control valve of
duty ratio control solenoid valve
占空比控制电磁阀型怠速控制阀

1、5—springs 弹簧；2—coil 线圈；
3—valve stem 阀杆；4—control valve 控制阀

# Unit 7　GASOLINE ENGINE COMPUTER-AIDED CONTROL SYSTEM

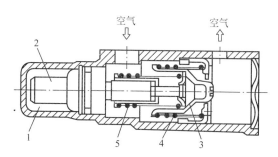

图 7.7　The fast idle control valve　快怠速控制阀

1—cooling fluid chamber 冷却液腔；2—paraffin temperature sensing element 石蜡感温元件；
3—control valve 控制阀；4、5—springs 弹簧

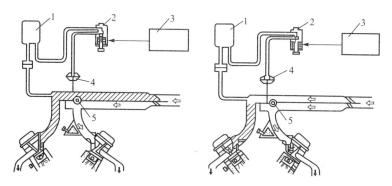

图 7.8　Power valve control system　动力阀控制系统

1—vacuum tank 真空罐；2—vacuum electromagnetic valve 真空电磁阀；
3—electronic control unit(ECU)电子控制单元；4—diaphragm vacuum
chamber 膜片真空室；5—power valve 动力阀

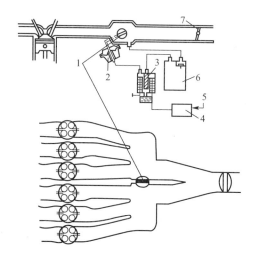

图 7.9　The harmonic inlet pressurization control system　谐波进气增压控制系统

1—inlet control valve 进气控制阀；2—vacuum actuator 真空驱动器；3—vacuum solenoid valve
真空电磁阀；4—ECU 电子控制单元；5—rotational speed signal 转速信号；
6—vacuum tank 真空罐；7—throttle 节气门

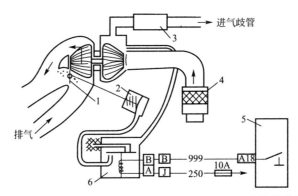

**图 7.10　The exhaust gas turbo pressurization control system　废气涡轮增压控制系统**
1—switching valve 切换阀；2—driving air chamber 驱动气室；3—air cooler 空气冷却器；4—air-filter 空气滤清器；5—ECU 电子控制单元；6—pressure release solenoid valve 释压电磁阀

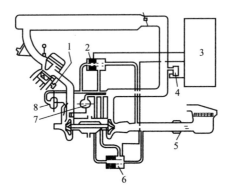

**图 7.11　The exhaust gas turbo pressurization rotating speed control system　废气涡轮增压器转速控制系统**
1—knock sensor 爆燃传感器；2—exchange valve control electromagnetic valve 切换阀控制电磁阀；3—ECU 电子控制单元；4—manifold absolute pressure sensor 进气管绝对压力传感器；5—air-flow sensor 空气流量传感器；6—injector control solenoid valve 喷油器控制电磁阀；7—injection ring drive air chamber 喷油器驱动气室；8—exchange valve drive chamber 切换阀驱动气室

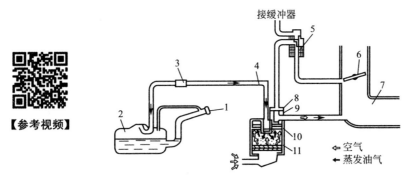

**图 7.12　The evaporative emission control system　废气排放控制系统**
1—fuel-tank cap 油箱盖；2—fuel tank 油箱；3—one-way valve 单向阀；4—exhaust manifold 排气管；5—electromagnetic valve 电磁阀；6—throttle 节气门；7—intake manifold 进气管；8—vacuum chamber 真空室；9—vacuum control valve 真空控制阀；10—quantification emission hole 定量排放孔；11—charcoal canister 活性炭罐

# Unit 7  GASOLINE ENGINE COMPUTER-AIDED CONTROL SYSTEM

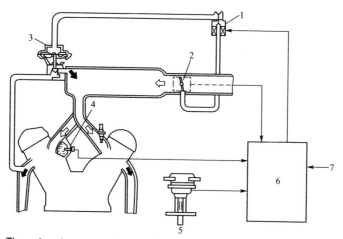

图 7.13  The exhaust gas recycle open-loop control system  废气再循环开环控制系统

1—exhaust gas recycle electromagnetic valve 废气再循环电磁阀；2—throttle 节气门；3—EGR valve 废气再循环阀；4—cooling water temperature sensor 冷却液温度传感器；5—crankshaft position sensor 曲轴位置传感器；6—ECU 电子控制单元；7—starting signal 起动信号

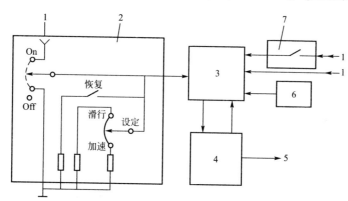

图 7.14  The cruise control system  巡航控制系统

1—power 电源；2—control switch 操纵开关；3—cruise control 巡航控制；4—actuating cell 执行元件；5—throttle 节气门；6—speed sensor 车速传感器；7—brake light switch 制动灯开关

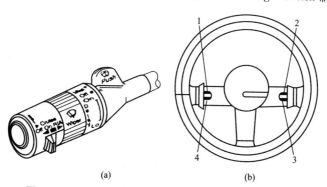

图 7.15  The cruise control switch  巡航控制操纵开关

(a) control switch on steering signal handle 操纵开关在转向信号手柄上；

(b) switch on steering wheel 操纵开关在转向盘上

1—set 设定；2—respond 回复；3—accelerating 加速；4—glide 滑行

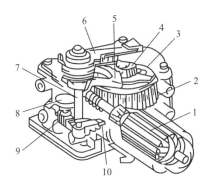

图 7.16　The cruise control actuator of electric motor　电动机式巡航控制执行元件

1—electric motor 电动机；2—magnetic clutch driving plate 电磁离合器主动盘；3—magnetic clutch driven plate 电磁离合器从动盘；4—retardation gear 减速齿轮；5—sector gear 扇齿轮；6—throttle control arm 节气门控制臂；7—output shaft 输出轴；8—throttle position sensor(TPS) 节气门位置传感器；9—TPS driving gear 节气门位置传感器驱动齿轮；
10—safety switch 安全开关

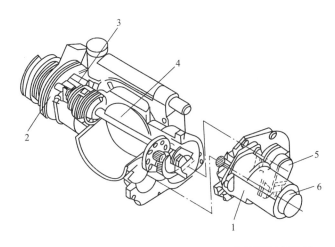

图 7.17　The electronic throttle system　电控节气门系统

1—magnetic clutch 电磁离合器；2—accelerator position sensor 加速踏板位置传感器；3—throttle control boom 节气门控制杆；4—throttle 节气门；5—throttle position sensor 节气门位置传感器；6—throttle controlling electric motor 节气门控制电动机

## Reading Materials

### Passage 1

#### Introduction of Gasoline Engine Computer-Aided Control System

Gasoline engine computer-aided control system mainly includes idle speed control system, inlet control system, pressure control system, emission control system, cruise control system and electronically controlled throttle system.

Idle speed control system function is the ECU (Electronic Control Unit) based on

# Unit 7  GASOLINE ENGINE COMPUTER-AIDED CONTROL SYSTEM

the engine operating temperature and load, which automatically control the intake flow rate on idle speed condition, maintaining the stability of engine idle speed.

Inlet control system is divided into power inlet valve control system and harmonic inlet pressurization control system.

Power inlet valve control system function is to control the size of air flow with engine inlet, to accommodate the different engine speed and load, and thereby improve engine power output.

Harmonic inlet pressurization control system function is changing the propagation distance of pressure wave inside intake manifold, according to engine speed changes, to increase volumetric efficiency, improving the engine performance.

Pressurization control system function is based on the size of the engine inlet air pressure to control the pressurization device work, which can control the inlet air pressure, improving engine power and economy.

Emission control system is mainly divided into gasoline vapor emission control system, exhaust gas recirculation control system, the secondary air supply system.

Gasoline vapor emission control system function is to collect gasoline vapor inside petrol tank and float bowl, which can be re-introduced into the cylinder to participate in combustion, prevent gasoline vapor directly into the atmosphere and cause pollution. At the same time, according to engine operating conditions, controlling the amount of gasoline steam in the combustion.

The function of exhaust gas recirculation control system is the proper quantity of exhaust gas re-introduction of the cylinder to participate in combustion, thereby reducing the maximum temperature inside the cylinder, in order to reduce $NO_x$ emissions.

The cruise control system is the ECU based on various sensor signals to determine vehicle operating conditions, through the implementation of the components automatically adjust throttle opening to make the car speed and configuration of the speed consistent.

 阅读材料

**材料1（参考译文）**

## 汽油发动机计算机辅助控制系统介绍

汽油发动机计算机辅助控制系统主要包括怠速控制系统、进气控制系统、压力控制系统、废气排放控制系统、巡航控制系统和电子控制节气门系统。

怠速控制系统的功能是基于对发动机的工作温度和负荷控制的电子控制单元，自动控制怠速条件下的进气流量，保持发动机怠速稳定。

进气控制系统分为电源进气阀控制系统和谐波增压进气控制系统。

电源进气阀控制系统的功能是控制发动机进气流量，以适应不同的发动机转速和负荷，从而提高发动机的功率输出。

谐波增压进气控制系统的功能是改变进气歧管中压力波的传播距离，根据发动机转速的变化，增加容积效率，提高发动机性能。

增压控制系统的功能是基于发动机进口空气压力，控制增压器工作，进而控制进口空气压力，改善发动机的动力性和经济性。

【参考视频】

废气排放控制系统主要分为汽油蒸气排放控制系统、废气再循环控制系统、二次空气供给系统。

汽油蒸气排放控制系统的功能是收集内汽油箱和浮子室的汽油蒸气，将这些蒸气重新引入气缸并燃烧，防止其直接污染大气。同时，根据发动机工况，控制燃烧中的汽油蒸气量。

【参考视频】

气体的废气再循环控制系统的功能是将废气重新引入到气缸并燃烧，从而降低气缸内的温度，以减少氮氧化物的排放。

巡航控制系统的电控单元根据各种传感器信号，了解组件的执行情况，自动调整节气门开度，使汽车的速度和速度配位一致。

材料2

## Emission Control System

The purpose of the emission control system is just that: it controls the emissions and exhaust from your vehicle. The idea is to turn the harmful gases your car manufactures into harmless ones that don't ruin the environment, or us. Some of the problem gases are: hydrocarbons, carbon monoxide, carbon dioxide, nitrogen oxides, sulfur dioxide, phosphorus, lead and other metals.

To help control these substances, some changes have been made in our gasoline to eliminate them. We also have developed ways to test emissions, which have caused automotive manufacturers to develop better, safer emission system. Although emission control system vary between manufacturers and vehicles, they all have the same goal and use many of the same methods. Emission controls have reduced carbon monoxide and hydrocarbon emissions by about ninety-six percent from precontrol vehicles. Hydrocarbons, carbon monoxide and oxides of nitrogen are created during the combustion process and are emitted into the atmosphere from the tail pipe. There are also hydrocarbons emitted as a result of vaporization of gasoline and from the crankcase of the automobile. The need to control the emissions from automobiles gave rise to the computerization of the automobile. An oxygen sensor was installed in the exhaust system and would measure the fuel content of the exhaust stream. It then would send a signal to a microprocessor, which would analyze the reading and operate a fuel mixture or air mixture device to create the proper air/fuel ratio. As computer systems progressed, there were able to adjust ignition sparking timing as well as operate the other emission controls that were installed on the vehicle. The computer is also capable of monitoring and diagnosing itself. Devices related

# Unit 7  GASOLINE ENGINE COMPUTER-AIDED CONTROL SYSTEM

to the emission control system installed on the automobile are: tailpipe, muffler, EGR (Exhaust Gas Recirculation) valve, catalytic converter, air pump, PCV (Positive Crankcase Ventilation) valve, and charcoal canister.

### Exhaust Manifold

The exhaust manifold, usually constructed of east iron, is a pipe that conducts the exhaust gases from the combustion chambers to the exhaust pipe. It has smooth curves in it for improving the flow of exhaust. The exhaust manifold is bolted to tile cylinder head.

### Exhaust Pipe

The exhaust pipe is the bent-up or convoluted pipes you will notice underneath your car. Some are shaped to go over the rear axle, allowing the rear axle to move up and down without bumping into the exhaust pipe; some are shaped to bend around under the floor of the ear, connecting the catalytic converter with the muffler.

### Muffler

Exhaust gases leave the engine under extremely high pressure. The pressure of the gases is reduced when they pass through the muffler, so they go out of the tail pipe quietly. The muffler is made of metal and is located underneath the body of the car. It's connected between the tail pipe and the catalytic converter.

### Tailpipe

The tailpipe is a long metal tube attached to the muffler. It discharges the exhaust gases from the muffler of your engine into the air outside the car.

### Dual Exhaust System

The advantage of a dual exhaust system is that the engine exhausts more freely, thereby lowering the back pressure which is inherent in an exhaust system. With a dual exhaust system, a sizable increase in engine horsepower can be obtained because the "breathing" capacity of the engine is improved, leaving less exhaust gases in the engine at the end of each exhaust stroke.

### Catalytic Converter

When your engine burns fuel, it produces gases that are bad for the environment. These noxious gases are hydrocarbons, carbon monoxide, and nitrogen oxides. To prevent the engine from polluting the environment with these gases, we include a catalytic converter in our emission systems. The catalytic converter is installed in the exhaust line, between the exhaust manifold and the muffler, and we make use of chemicals that act a catalyst. In the ease of the catalytic converter, the chemicals cause a reaction in the pollutants in the exhaust. The converter is lined with chemicals such as aluminum oxide, platinum and palladium. These chemicals cause the carbon monoxide and hydrocarbons to change into water vapor and carbon dioxide. Some converters have a third lining of chemicals, platinum and rhodium. That reduce nitrogen oxides(three-way, dual bed converter).

### PCV Valve

The process of combustion forms several gases and vapors; many of them are quite corrosive. Some of these gases get past the piston rings and into the crankcase. If left in the crankcase, these substances would cause all kinds of bad things(rust, corrosion, and formation of sludge), so they have to be removed. The PCV system uses a hose connected between the engine and the intake manifold. The purpose of the positive crankcase ventilation(PCV)system is to take the vapors produced in the crankcase during the normal combustion process and redirect them into the air/fuel intake system to be burned during combustion.

### EGR Valve

The exhaust gas recirculation(EGR)valve is used to send some of the exhaust gas back into the cylinders to reduce combustion temperature. Nitrous oxides (nasty pollutants)form when the combustion temperature gets above 2,500 degrees °F. This happens, at such temperatures when the nitrogen in the air mixes with the oxygen to create nitrous oxides, which the sun hits will turn into smog. The EGR valve tries to prevent this. By recirculating some of the exhaust gas back through the intake manifold to the cylinders, which dilutes the air/fuel mixture so as to lower the combustion chamber temperature. Lowering the combustion temperature lowers the amount of nitrous oxide produced. Consequently, less of it comes out of the tailpipe.

### Evaporative Controls

Gasoline evaporates quite easily. 20% of all HC emissions from automobile are from the gas tank. An evaporative control system was developed to eliminate this source of pollution. The function of the fuel evaporative control system is to trap and store evaporative emissions from the gas tank and carburetor. A charcoal canister is used to trap the fuel evaporation.

### Air Injection

Since no internal combustion engine is 100% efficient, there will always be some unburned fuel in the exhaust. This increases hydrocarbon emissions. To eliminate this source of emissions an air injection system was created. Combustion requires fuel, oxygen and heat. Without any one of the three, combustion cannot occur. Inside the exhaust manifold there is sufficient heat to support combustion, if we introduce some oxygen, then any unburned fuel will ignite. This combustion will not produce any power, but it will reduce excessive hydrocarbon emissions. Unlike in the combustion chamber, this combustion is uncontrolled, so if the fuel content of the exhaust is excessive, explosions,

## Unit 7　GASOLINE ENGINE COMPUTER-AIDED CONTROL SYSTEM

which sound like popping, will occur. There are times when under normal conditions, such as deceleration, the fuel content is excessive. Under these conditions we would want to shut off the air injection system. This is accomplished through the use of a diverter valve, which instead of shutting the air pump off, diverts the air away from the exhaust manifold. Since all of this is done after the combustion process is complete, this is one emission control that has no effect on engine performance. The only maintenance that is required is a careful inspection of the air pump drive belt.

**材料2（参考译文）**

### 废气排放控制系统

废气排放控制系统的作用是控制汽车尾气排放物。使用排放控制装置的目的是将汽车产生的有害气体转化为不破坏环境且无害于人类的气体。这些有害气体是：碳氢化合物（未燃）、一氧化碳、二氧化碳、氮氧化物、二氧化硫、磷、铅及其他金属。

为了帮助控制这些物质，我们已经对汽油成分进行了改进，以消除有害排放。我们也制定了相应的排放检测方法，这也促使汽车厂商开发更好、更环保的废气排放控制系统。虽然排放控制系统会随着厂商和车辆的不同而有所差别，但它们的作用都是相同的，且多数使用相同的方法。与未安装排放控制系统的汽车相比，装有排放控制系统的汽车可以将一氧化碳和碳氢化合物排放降低96%。碳氢化合物、一氧化碳和氮氧化物是在燃烧过程中产生的，并通过排气管排到大气中，也有一些碳氢化合物是以汽油蒸发和从曲轴箱中窜入大气的形式排放的。对汽车排放控制的需要促进了汽车的计算机控制化。在排气系统中安装了氧气传感器，用于测量废气流中的氧含量。氧气传感器将信号传给微处理机，微处理机分析读数并控制燃油、空气混合装置以便获得正确的空燃比。当计算机系统运行时，计算机可以像控制其他安装在车辆上的排放装置一样调整点火时刻，计算机同时能够自我检测和诊断。安装在汽车上与排放系统有关的装置有：排气尾管、消声器、EGR（废气再循环）阀、催化转换器空气泵、PCV（曲轴箱强制通风）阀及活性炭罐等。

### 排气歧管

材料通常为铸铁的排气歧管是将废气从燃烧室引进排气管的管道，其内部流线结构改善了排气流。排气歧管用螺栓连接固定在气缸盖上。

### 排气管

排气管是我们在汽车底部看到的弯曲或盘旋的管道。有些是做成一定形状，穿越过后桥之上，这样，后桥上下运动时就不会触及排气管；有些是在汽车底板下方，连接催化转换器和消声器。

### 消声器

废气在非常高的压力下排出发动机。气体经过消声器后，压力减小，所以排出排气尾管时很安静。消声器用金属材料制造，被安装在车身底部，连接在排气尾管和催化转换器之间。

### 排气尾管

排气尾管是安装在消声器后的长金属管。排气尾管将流经消声器的发动机废气排到汽车外面的大气中。

### 双排气系统

双排气系统的优点是使发动机排气更加顺畅，因此降低了单排气系统中固有的背压。使用双排气系统后，大大增加了发动机的功率。这是因为双排气系统使得每个排气冲程终了时留在发动机内的残余废气减少，从而增大了发动机进气量。

### 催化转换器

【参考视频】

当发动机燃烧燃油时，它产生有害于环境的废气。这些有害气体是碳氢化合物、一氧化碳、氮氧化物。为了防止发动机排放的这些气体污染环境，排放系统里安装了催化转换器。催化转换器安装在排气管内，位于排气歧管和消声器之间，利用化学物质作为催化剂。催化转换器内的化学物质使得排气中的有害物质发生反应。催化转换器内涂有氧化铝、铂和钯等化学物质层，这些化学物质层将一氧化碳和碳氢化合物转化成水蒸气和二氧化碳。有些催化转换器内还有第三种化学物质层：铂和铑，这种催化剂能减少氮氧化合物(三元、双层转化器)。

### PCV 阀

【参考视频】

燃烧过程会生成多种气体和蒸汽，其中有很多气体是具有腐蚀性，有些气体经过活塞环进入到曲轴箱内。如果这些燃烧产生物停留在曲轴箱内，会产生各种副作用(如锈蚀、腐蚀及生成油泥)，因此，必须将它们清除。用橡胶软管将PCV系统连接在发动机和进气歧管之间。曲轴箱强制通风装置(PCV)的作用是将正常燃烧过程中曲轴箱产生的油气改道引入可燃混合气的进气系统中以便燃烧。

### EGR 阀

废气再循环(EGR)阀将一部分废气引入到气缸内，用于降低燃烧温度。氮氧化物(有害污染物)在燃烧温度超过华氏2500度时产生。在高温时，空气中氮与氧混合后生成氮氧化物，它遇到太阳照射后将变成烟幕。EGR阀用于阻止氮氧化物的产生，通过将部分废气重新经进气歧管引入到气缸，废气冲稀了可燃混合气，从而降低了燃烧室温度。降低了燃烧室温度就降低了氮氧化物的生成量，因此降低了经排气尾管的氮氧化物排放量。

### 蒸发控制

汽油非常容易蒸发。20%的汽车碳氢化合物的排放来自油箱蒸发排放，所以研制出了蒸发控制装置来消除这种污染源。燃油蒸发控制系统的作用是收集和存储来自油箱的蒸发排放。活性炭罐用于收集燃油蒸发物。

### 空气喷射

由于没有一个内燃机的工作效率是100%，因而在排气中总会存在未燃烧的燃油。这

## Unit 7  GASOLINE ENGINE COMPUTER-AIDED CONTROL SYSTEM

导致了碳氢化合物排放的增加。为了消除这种类型的碳氢排放，空气喷射系统应运而生。燃烧需要燃油、氧气和热量，三者缺一，燃烧都不会发生。在排气歧管内有足够的热量引起燃烧，若引入一些氧气，则未燃烧的燃油就能燃烧。这种燃烧不做任何功，但会降低很多的碳氢排放。和燃烧室内的燃烧不同，排气歧管内的燃烧是不被控制的。所以如果排气中燃油过多，则燃烧将以爆炸的形式进行，并产生爆裂声。在某些正常工况下，如减速，排气中燃油含量将过多。此时我们希望关闭空气喷射系统。通过使用转向阀，而不是关闭空气泵，可将空气从排气歧管中引出。因为所有这些都是在燃烧过程完成后进行的，所以这种排放控制方法对发动机性能无任何影响，唯一需要注意的是：认真检查空气泵驱动传动带。

# Unit 8

# FUEL SUPPLY SYSTEM FOR DIESEL ENGINE
# 柴油发动机燃料供给系统

【参考视频】

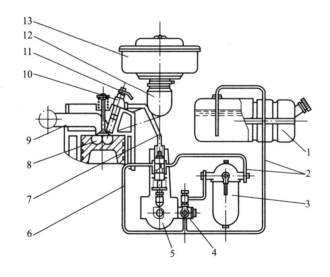

图 8.1  Fuel supply system for diesel engine  柴油发动机燃料供给系统

1—diesel tank 柴油箱；2—low pressure pipe 低压油管；3—oil filter 柴油滤清器；
4—feed pump 输油泵；5—injection pump 喷油泵；6—return pipe 回油管；
7—high pressure pipe 高压油管；8—combustion chamber 燃烧室；
9—exhaust pipe 排气管；10—valve 气门；11—injector 喷油器；
12—induction pipe 进气管；13—air filter 空气滤清器

# Unit 8 FUEL SUPPLY SYSTEM FOR DIESEL ENGINE

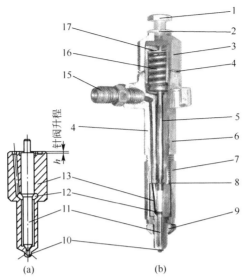

图 8.2 Hole type injector 孔式喷油器

(a) nozzle 喷嘴;(b) injector 喷油器

1—fuel return pipe screw 回油管螺钉;2—fuel return gasket 回油管垫片;3—pressure-regulator screw cap 调压螺钉护帽;4—gasket 垫片;5—eject rod 顶杆;6—injector housing 喷油器体;7—fastening screw cap 紧固螺套;8—dowel 定位销;9—nozzle gasket 喷嘴垫;10—injection hole 喷孔;11—pintle valve 针阀;12—ring body 环形油腔;13—pintle valve housing 针阀体;14—fuel inlet gallery 进油道;15—fuel inlet joint 进油管接头;16—pressure-regulator spring 调压弹簧;17—pressure-regulator screw 调压螺钉

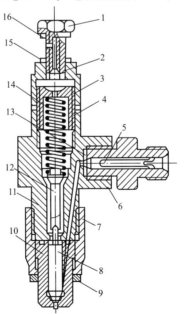

图 8.3 Pintle type injector 轴针式喷油器

1—return oil pipe screw 回油管螺钉;2—pressure-regulator screw cap 调压螺钉护帽;3—pressure-regulator screw 调压螺钉;4、9、15、16—washer 垫圈;5—filter core 滤芯;6—oil inlet joint 进油管接头;7—fastening screw cap 紧固螺套;8—pintle valve 针阀;10—pintle valve housing 针阀体;11—injector body 喷油器体;12—eject rod 顶杆;13—washer 垫圈;14—pressure-regulator spring 调压弹簧

【参考图文】

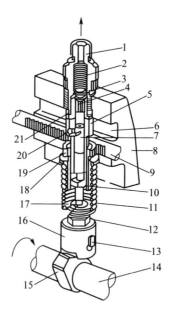

图 8.4　Injection pump　喷油泵

1—delivery valve holder 出油阀紧座；2—delivery valve spring 出油阀弹簧；3—delivery valve 出油阀；
4—delivery valve seat 出油阀座；5—plunger collar 柱塞套；6—low pressure fuel body 低压油腔；
7—plunger 柱塞；8—injection pump housing 喷油泵体；9—fuel adjusting screw 油量调节螺杆；
10—fuel adjusting sleeve 油量调节套筒；11—plunger spring 柱塞弹簧；12—fuel supply timing adjusting screw 供油正时调节螺钉；13—positioning slide 定位滑块；14—camshaft 凸轮轴；
15—cam 凸轮；16—cylinder components 挺柱体部件；17—plunger spring under seat 柱塞弹簧下座；18—plunger spring over seat 柱塞弹簧上座；19—ring gear 齿圈；
20—into oil return hole 进回油孔；21—seal washer 密封垫

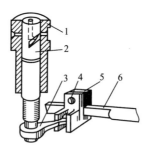

图 8.5　Fork(connecting rod)fuel adjusting structure　拨叉拉杆式油量调节机构

1—plunger collar 柱塞套；2—plunger 柱塞；3—plunger adjusting arm 柱塞调节臂；
4—fork fastening screw 拨叉紧固螺钉；5—fork 拨叉；
6—fuel-supply connecting rod 供油拉杆

## Unit 8  FUEL SUPPLY SYSTEM FOR DIESEL ENGINE

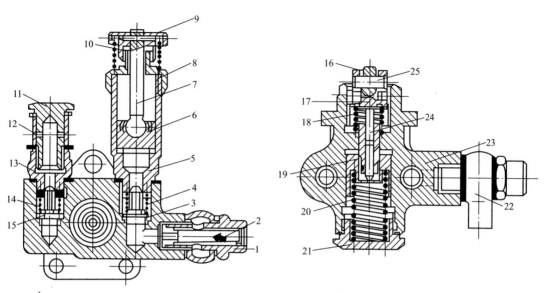

图 8.6  Piston fuel pump  活塞式输油泵

1—fuel inlet connection screw 进油管接头螺钉；2—strainer 滤网；3—intake valve 进油阀；4—intake valve spring 进油阀弹簧；5—pump housing 泵体；6—pump piston 泵活塞；7—pump rod 泵杆；8—pump cap 泵盖；9—pump pin 泵销；10—pump handle 泵柄；11—fuel outlet joint screw sleeve 出油管接头螺套；12—boot 保护套；13—pipe joint 油管接头；14—processing valve spring 出油阀弹簧；15—delivery valve 出油阀；16—roller 滚轮；17—roller shelf 滚轮架；18—roller spring 滚轮弹簧；19—piston 活塞；20—piston spring 活塞弹簧；21—plug 螺塞；22—fuel inlet joint 进油管接头；23—pump housing 泵体；24—eject rod 顶杆；25—roller pin 滚轮销

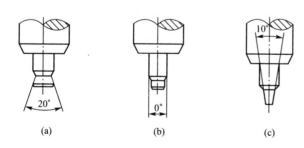

图 8.7  Head for pintle type nozzle valve  轴针式喷油嘴针阀头部形状

(a) inverted cone 倒锥；(b) cylinder 圆柱；(c) clockwise cone 顺锥

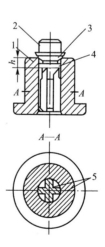

图 8.8  Delivery valve  出油阀偶件

1—outlet valve seat 出油阀座；2—delivery valve 出油阀；3—seal cone 密封锥面；4—bleed ring 减压环带；5—cross-shape slotting 十字切槽

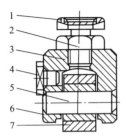

图 8.9　Screw regulating lifter units
螺钉调节式挺柱体部件

1—regulating screw 调整螺钉；2—lock nut 锁紧螺母；3—cylinder 挺柱体；4—guide sliding block 导向滑块；5—roller pin 滚轮销；6—roller bushing 滚轮衬套；7—roller 滚轮

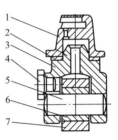

图 8.10　Block regulating lifter units
垫块调节式挺柱体部件

1—plunger spring seat 柱塞弹簧座；2—regulating gasket 调整垫片；3—cylinder 挺柱体；4—guide sliding block 导向滑块；5—roller pin 滚轮销；6—roller bushing 滚轮衬套；7—roller 滚轮

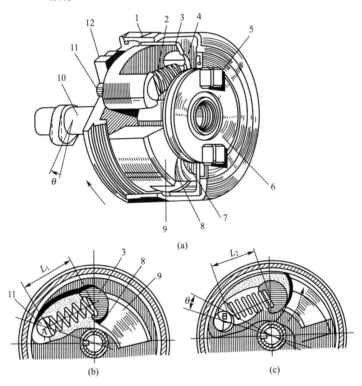

图 8.11　SA type fuel injection advance device SA 型喷油提前器

（a）advance unit 提前器单元；（b）initial position 起始位置；（c）ultimate position 终了位置

1—shield cover 防护罩；2—advancer spring 提前器弹簧；3—driving pin 传动销；4—actuating disc 主动盘；5—drive pawl 传动爪；6—actuating disc flange 主动盘凸缘；7—driving pin 传动销；8—flyweight novikov surface 飞锤圆弧面；9—flyweight 飞锤；10—injection pump camshaft 喷油泵凸轮轴；11—flyweight pin 飞锤销；12—driven disc 从动盘

$L_1$—initial position of spring 弹簧起始位置；$L_2$—ultimate position of spring 弹簧终了位置；
$\theta$—advance angle regulating range 提前角调节范围

## Unit 8　FUEL SUPPLY SYSTEM FOR DIESEL ENGINE

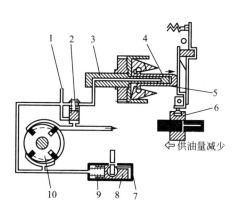

图 8.12　Load sensing fuel supply advancer
负荷传感供油提前装置

1—fuel inlet 进油口；2—pressure-regulator valve 调压阀；3—speed governor shaft 调速器轴；4—speed governor sleeve 调速套筒；5—fuel drain hole 泄油量孔；6—fuel control sleeve 油量调节套筒；7—pump housing 泵体；8—injection advancer piston 喷油提前器活塞；9—spring 弹簧；10—sliding vane feed pump 滑片式输油泵

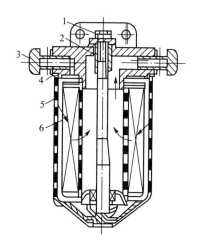

图 8.13　Single diesel filter　单级柴油滤清器
1—bleed screw 放气螺钉；2—central bolt 中心螺栓；3—oil pipe joint 油管接头；4—filter cap 滤清器盖；5—housing 壳体；6—filter core 滤芯

## Reading Materials

Passage 1

### Introduction of the Fuel Supply System for Diesel Engine

Diesel engines are used on some cars and light trucks. The diesel engine uses the heat of compression, instead of a spark plug, to ignite the fuel. Diesel fuel injection is similar to gasoline injection, but requires higher injection pressures. Air is drawn into the cylinder and highly compressed. The compression is so high that the compressed air will reach temperatures of 1000°F(538.2°C). At the precise time the piston has completed the compression stroke, diesel fuel is sprayed into the combustion chamber, or an offset prechamber. The intense heat of the compressed air ignites the fuel, and the power stroke follows.

The diesel oil was sucked from the fuel tank and pumped into the filter by the fuel feed pump. The filter removed the impurities, then the diesel fuel entered the fuel injection pump. The high-pressurized diesel fuel came from the fuel injection pump entered injector(injection nozzle) through high-pressurized line. The excess oil returned to the fuel tank by leakage return pipe.

 阅读材料

**材料 1（参考译文）**

**柴油机供油系统介绍**

柴油发动机一般用在一些轿车和轻型货车上。柴油发动机使用压缩热能，而不是通过火花塞点燃燃料。柴油机燃油喷射与汽油喷射类似，但需要较高的喷射压力。空气卷入气缸并被高度压缩，压缩空气可达到华氏 1000 度（摄氏 538.2℃）。在精确的时间完成了活塞压缩行程后，柴油燃料喷入燃烧室或偏移预燃室，压缩空气的高热点燃燃料，紧接着是做功行程。

柴油是从油箱吸出来的，由燃油泵传送给过滤器，经过滤器去除杂质，然后进入喷油泵。高压柴油燃料来自燃油喷射泵，通过高压管进入喷油器。过剩的燃油通过回油管流回油箱。

Passage 2

**How the Fuel Supply System for Diesel Engine Works**

The diesel engine draws only air in during the suction stroke. During the compression stroke this air is heated to such a high temperature that the diesel fuel injected into the engine toward the end of the compression stroke ignites of its own accord. The fuel is metered by the fuel injection pump and is injected under high pressure through the injection nozzle into the combustion chamber.

Fuel injection must take place:

(1) in an accurately metered quantity corresponding to the engine load;

(2) at the correct instant in time;

(3) for a precisely determined period of time;

(4) in a manner suited to the particular combustion process concerned.

More and more demands are being made on the diesel engine's injection system as a result of the severe regulations governing exhaust and noise emission, and the demand for lower fuel-consumption. Basically speaking, depending on the particular diesel combustion process (direct or indirect injection) in order to ensure efficient air/fuel mixture formation, the injection system must inject the fuel into the combustion chamber at a pressure between 350 and 2,050 bar, and the injection fuel quantity must be metered with extreme accuracy.

The mechanical (flywheel) governing principle for diesel injection system is increasingly being superseded by the electronic diesel control(EDC). In the passenger car

# Unit 8　FUEL SUPPLY SYSTEM FOR DIESEL ENGINE

and commercial vehicle sector, new diesel fuel-injection systems are all EDC-controlled.

### Fuel Injection Pump

Diesel in-line injection pumps and distributor injection pumps are the two types of fuel injection pumps.

### In-line Fuel-injection Pump

All in-line fuel-injection pumps have a plunger-and-barrel assembly for each cylinder. As the name implies, this comprises the pump barrel and corresponding plunger. The pump camshaft, integrated in the pump and driven by the engine, forces the pump plunger in the delivery direction. The plunger is returned by its spring.

The plunger-and-barrel assemblies are arranged in-line, and plunger lift cannot be varied. In order to permit changes in the delivery quantity, slots have been machined into the plunger, the diagonal edges of which are known as helixes. When the plunger is rotated by the movable control rack, the helixes permit the selection of the required effective stroke. Depending upon the fuel-injection conditions, delivery valves are installed between the pump's pressure chamber and the fuel-injection lines. These not only precisely terminate the injection process and prevent secondary injection(dribble) at the nozzle, but also ensure a family of uniform pump characteristic curves.

### Distributor Fuel-Injection Pump

Distributor pumps have a mechanical(flywheel) governor, or an electronic control with integrated timing device. The distributor pump has only one plunger-and-barrel assembly for all the engine's cylinders.

### Axial-piston distributor pump

In the case of the axial-piston distributor pump, fuel is supplied by a vane-type pump. Pressure generation, distribution to the individual engine cylinders, is the job of a central piston which runs on a cam plate. For one revolution of the driveshaft, the piston performs as many strokes as there are engine cylinders. The rotating-reciprocating movement is imparted to the plunger by the cams on the under side of the cam plate which ride on the rollers of the roller ring.

On the conventional VE axial-piston distributor pump with mechanical(flywheel) governor, or electronically controlled actuator, a control collar defines the fuel quantity. The pump's start of delivery can be adjusted by the roller ring(timing device). On the conventional solenoid-valve-controlled axial-piston distributor pump, instead of a control collar an electronically controlled high-pressure solenoid valve controls the injected fuel quantity. The open and closed-loop control signals are processed in two ECUs. Speed is controlled by appropriate triggering of the actuator.

### Radial-piston distributor pump

In the case of the radial-piston distributor pump, fuel is supplied by a vane-type pump. A radial piston pump with cam ring and two to four radial pistons is responsible for generation of the high pressure and for fuel delivery. The injected fuel quantity is metered by a high-pressure solenoid valve. The timing device rotates the cam ring in order to adjust the start of delivery. As is the case with the solenoid-valve-controlled axial piston pump, all open and closed-loop control signals are processed in two ECUs. Speed is controlled by appropriate triggering of the actuator.

### Injection Nozzles

The injection nozzles and their respective nozzle holders are vitally important components situated between the injection pump and the diesel engine. Injection nozzles serve to feed and atomize the fuel injected into the cylinders of engine. The main parts of nozzles are the nozzle needle and the nozzle body. They affected the performance of injection nozzles greatly. Nozzle should be optimized for the particular engine. This means optimum combustion, minimal pollution emissions and full engine output. Pintle nozzles are used with in-line injection pumps on indirect-injection(IDI) engines. The nozzle body of this type nozzle has only one hole, and the needle protrudes from the nozzle body. Hole-type nozzles are used with in-line injection pumps on direct-injection(DI) engines. There are several holes on the nozzle body, usually two to five holes. The nozzle body of this type nozzle has only one hole, and the needle stays inside the nozzle body all the time.

## 材料2（参考译文）

### 柴油机燃料供给系统的工作原理

柴油发动机只在进气行程中吸入空气。在压缩行程中，空气被加热到很高的温度，以致注入的柴油发动机燃油在压缩行程结束时自行点燃。这种燃油由燃油喷射泵计量，在高压下通过喷嘴进入燃烧室。

燃油喷射在下列条件下发生：

（1）准确计量相应的发动机负荷；

（2）正确的时刻；

（3）精确确定的时间段；

（4）适合燃烧过程有关的特殊方式。

由于制定了严格的废气和噪声排放规定，人们对柴油发动机喷射系统以及低油耗提出越来越高的要求。从根本上来说，它取决于某种特定的柴油燃烧过程（直接或间接喷射），以确保形成高效率空气/燃油混合气。喷射系统必须在350～2050bar压力下，把燃油注入燃烧室，燃油喷射量必须非常精确。

柴油喷射系统的机械（飞轮）工作原理逐渐地被柴油机控制系统（EDC）所取代。在乘

# Unit 8　FUEL SUPPLY SYSTEM FOR DIESEL ENGINE

用车和商用车领域，新的燃油喷射系统都是 EDC 控制的。

**喷油泵**

柴油泵包括柱塞式燃油喷射泵和分配式燃油喷射泵两种类型。

**柱塞式燃油喷射泵**

所有柱塞式燃油喷射泵的气缸都有柱塞偶件。顾名思义，这包括泵筒和相对应的柱塞。泵凸轮轴由泵集成组成，由发动机驱动，使得泵柱塞朝运油方向施力，弹簧使柱塞返回。

柱塞偶件是柱形排列的，柱塞移动不能更改。为了允许传送量的变化，柱塞中安装了槽，它的对角线边缘是螺旋形状的。当柱塞由移动控制架旋转时，螺旋形状有助于有效行程，以选择燃油喷射条件。在泵压力室和燃油喷射柱之间安装了出油阀，这不仅终止了喷射过程，防止喷嘴的二次喷射，而且还确保了泵特性曲线的统一。

**分配式燃油喷射泵**

分配式泵由机械调速器或有定时装置的集成电子控制。分配式泵的发动机气缸中只有一个柱塞偶件。

**轴向活塞分配式喷油泵**

轴向活塞中是由片式泵供应燃油的。压力的产生并分配给每个的发动机气缸的任务是由一个在凸轮板上的中央活塞完成的。对于驱动轴的运转，由于有发动机气缸，所以活塞执行尽可能多的行程。

传统 VE 型轴向活塞分配式喷油泵带有机械调速器（飞轮）或电控致动器，由控制环控制喷油量，并由滚圈（计时装置）调节传输。然而，传统电磁阀控制的轴向活塞分配式喷油泵却是由电控高压电磁阀控制喷油量。开环和闭环信号由两个 ECU 控制，速度由致动器的适时触发控制。

**径向活塞分配式喷油泵**

在径向活塞分配式喷油泵中，燃油是由叶片式泵供应的。带有凸轮环以及 2～4 个径向活塞的径向柱塞泵产生高压燃油并且负责燃油传送。注入的燃油量是由高压电磁阀计量的。调速装置旋转凸轮环用来调整首次传送。如同电磁阀控制的轴向活塞泵，所有打开和闭环控制信号是由两个电子控制单元处理的。速度是由适当的执行器触发控制的。

**喷嘴**

喷射喷嘴和喷嘴座位于喷油泵和柴油发动机之间，是极为重要的组成部分。喷射喷嘴可以注入和雾化注入发动机气缸中的燃料。喷嘴主要是由喷嘴针和喷嘴体组成，它们在很大程度上影响喷嘴的性能。针对不同的发动机应该优化喷嘴，这意味着最佳的燃烧，污染排放量最小，发动机输出功率最大。轴针式喷嘴用于间接喷射发动机上的柱塞式喷油泵。这种喷嘴的喷嘴体只有一个洞，喷嘴针从喷嘴体中突出来。孔式喷嘴用于直接喷射发动机上的柱塞式喷油泵，喷嘴体上通常有 2～5 个孔。这种喷嘴的喷嘴体也只有一个洞，而且喷嘴针一直处在喷嘴体中。

# Unit 9

# AUTOMOBILE COOLING SYSTEM
# 汽车冷却系统

【参考视频】

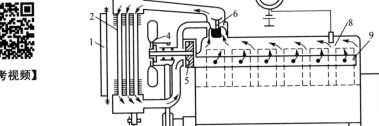

图 9.1 Components of water cooling system 水冷却系统的组成
1—louver 百叶窗；2—radiator 散热器；3—radiator cap 散热器盖；4—fan 风扇；5—pump 水泵；
6—thermostat 节温器；7—water temperature gauge 冷却液温度表；8—water jacket of
cylinder head 气缸盖水套；9—water distribution pipe 分水管；10—outlet valve 放水阀

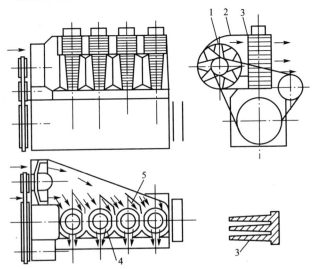

图 9.2 Components of air cooling system 风冷却系统的组成
1—fan 风扇；2—fan cowl 导流罩；3—radiator 散热片；4—cylinder cowl 气缸导流罩；5—shunt 分流板

# Unit 9　AUTOMOBILE COOLING SYSTEM

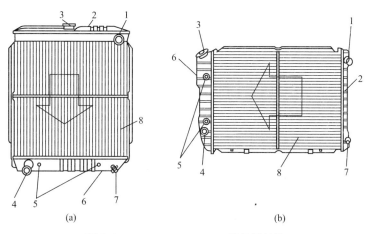

图 9.3　Structure of radiator 散热器结构

(a) down flow 竖流式；(b) cross flow 横流式

1—water inlet 进水口；2—inlet tank 进水室；3—radiator cap 散热器盖；4—water outlet 出水口；
5—inlet and outlet of transmission-fluid cooler 变速器油冷却器进、出口；6—outlet tank 出水室；
7—outlet valve 放水阀；8—radiator 散热器

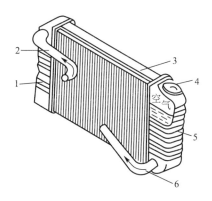

图 9.4　Cross flow radiator　横流式散热器

1—left water-reserve tank 左储水室；2—inlet pipe 进水管；3—radiator core 散热器芯；
4—radiator cap 散热器盖；5—right water-reserve tank 右储水室；6—outlet pipe 出水管

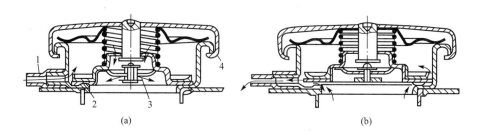

图 9.5　Structure of radiator cap 散热器盖的结构

（a）air valve opening 空气阀打开；(b) steam valve opening 蒸汽阀打开

1—vent valve 通气管；2—steam valve 蒸汽阀；3—air valve 空气阀；4—radiator cap 散热器盖

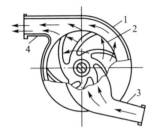

图9.6 Centrifugal water pump 离心式水泵
1—water pump shell 水泵壳体；2—impeller 叶轮；
3—water inlet 进水口；4—water outlet 出水口

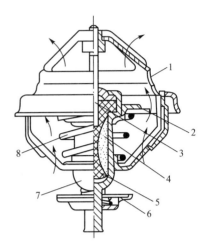

图9.7 Structure of wax-element thermostat
蜡式节温器的结构
1—anchor 支架；2—main valve 主阀门；
3—push rod 推杆；4—wax 石蜡；
5—tube 胶管；6—secondary valve
副阀门；7—thermostat housing
节温器壳体；8—spring 弹簧

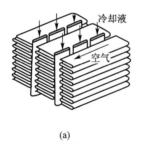 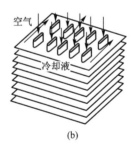

图9.8 Radiator core 散热器芯
(a) pipe-disc 管片式；(b) pipe-way 管带式

## Reading Materials

Passage 1

### Automobile Cooling System

An automobile's cooling system is the collection of parts and substances (coolants) that work together to maintain the engine's temperature at optimal levels. Comprising many different components such as water pump, coolant, a thermostat, etc., the system enables smooth and efficient functioning of the engine at the same time protecting it from damage.

# Unit 9　AUTOMOBILE COOLING SYSTEM

　　While it's running, an automobile's engine generates enormous amounts of heat. Each combustion cycle entails thousands of controlled explosions taking place every minute inside the engine. If the automobile races on and the heat generated within isn't dissipated, it would cause the engine to self-destruct. Hence, it is imperative to concurrently remove the waste heat. While the waste heat is also dissipated through the intake of cool air and exit of hot exhaust gases, the engine's cooling system is explicitly meant to keep the temperature within limits.

　　The cooling system essentially comprises passages inside the engine block and heads, a pump to circulate the coolant, a thermostat to control the flow of the coolant, a radiator to cool the coolant and a radiator cap controls the pressure within the system.

　　In order to achieve the cooling action, the system circulates the liquid coolant through passages in the engine block and heads. As it runs through, the coolant absorbs heat before returning to the radiator, to be cooled itself. Next, the cooled down coolant is recirculated and the cycle continues to maintain the engine's temperature at the right levels.

阅读材料

## 材料1（参考译文）

### 汽车冷却系统

　　汽车冷却系统由部件和物质（冷却液）组成，通过共同作用将发动机的温度保持在最佳水平。汽车冷却系统包括水泵、冷却液、恒温器等组件，使发动机能够顺利且有效地运作，同时使其免受损害。

　　汽车发动机运行时，会产生大量热量。在每个燃烧循环过程，发动机每分钟发生的控制爆破高达上千次。如果汽车快速行进而内存热量得不到消退，则会损坏发动机，因此，必须消除余热。排出的热量通过冷热空气得以消退，发动机的冷却系统将发动机的温度保持在限制范围内。

　　冷却系统主要包括发动机气缸体和气缸盖、水泵、恒温器、散热器和散热器盖。水泵用来冷却液循环；恒温器用来控制冷却液流量；散热器用来冷却冷却液；散热器盖用来控制系统内压力。

　　发动机通过循环缸体和缸盖通道的冷却剂实现冷却功能。运行时，返回散热器之前冷却剂吸收热量，自身冷却，然后，冷却液冷却，并且周期循环继续将发动机的温度保持在适当的水平。

Passage 2

### Engine Cooling System Components

　　A number of different constituents enable smooth operation of the automobile's cooling system. Some of the most essential ones are explained below.

### Engine Cooling Fluids

An engine coolant is a fluid which flows through the engine and prevents it from overheating by transferring the heat generated by the engine to other components that either make use of it or dissipate it. Features of an ideal coolant include high viscosity, thermal capacity, chemical inertness and low-cost. Further, it should neither cause nor promote corrosion of the cooling system.

### Water Cooling Systems

A water cooling system accomplishes the cooling action with the help of water. There are various components that make up the cooling system are the air blower, cooling fans, radiator pressure caps, water pipes, coolant hoses, radiator parts, radiators and water pumps. Each of these components plays an essential role. For instance, the radiator cools the coolant so that it can be reused, the water pump pumps the coolant through the system via water pipes, the air blower draws air through the radiator to achieve the cooling action, etc.

### Valves

The cooling system valves have an essential role to play. An engine's cooling system for an internal combustion engine utilizing liquid coolant, includes a liquid coolant filled radiator and engine "water" jacket, a radiator cap to pressurize the radiator, a coolant pump and a thermostat. While the thermostat determines when it is appropriate to either prohibit coolant flow or to allow coolant flow between the engine or radiator, the valve assembly acts like a door that opens up and closes as required.

### Cooling System Gaskets

The cooling system for engines include a cylinder block defining a water jacket within it, which has an inlet. Further, a water pump housing is attached to the cylinder block, and a water pump suction cover is fixed to the housing and sealed upon it by a gasket. The gasket plays an important role of projecting the water into the water jacket inlet so as to guide water within the system.

### Aluminum Housing

A water pump housing entails a construction that supports the casing of a driven water pump within the cooling system. The housing plays the vital role of installing the pump and keeping it in position.

### Buying Tips

(1) Always prefer new auto parts instead of used ones.

(2) Choose your suppliers carefully., establish a reasonable level of trust towards a supplier, through referrals, testimonial, or certifications.

# Unit 9  AUTOMOBILE COOLING SYSTEM

(3) Be wary of suppliers offering products at extraordinarily low prices.

(4) Ensure the specifics of the products you require from the supplier, before placing the order, a sample inspection is often the best way to do it.

(5) You need to understand the terms and conditions including warranties and guarantees associated with the supplies you order.

**材料2（参考译文）**

### 发动机冷却系统部件

汽车内部众多组件使冷却系统能够顺利运作，主要组成部分如下。

**发动机冷却液**

发动机冷却液是一种流经发动机的液体，用来防止由发动机产生的热量转移到其他部件从而导致过热。这些冷却液要么利用热量，要么将热量驱散。一种理想的冷却液应具备高黏度、热容量、化学惰性、低成本等优点，此外，也不会引起或加速冷却系统的腐蚀。

**水冷却系统**

水冷却系统在水的帮助下完成冷却。水冷却系统的组件分别是风机、冷却风扇、散热器高压帽、水管、冷却软管、散热器配件、散热器和水泵。每个组件都起着至关重要的作用。例如，散热器将冷却液冷却，以便重复使用；通过冷却水管道系统，水泵泵出冷却液；风机使空气流经散热器以达到降温目的。

**阀门**

冷却系统阀门具有重要作用。发动冷却系统包括充斥散热器和发动机水套的冷却液，用来为散热器加压的散热器高压帽，冷却液泵和恒温器。恒温器决定着冷却液流动或者发动机和散热器之间冷却液流动的时间，阀门总成如同门一样按要求开启或者关闭。

**冷却系统密封垫片**

发动机的冷却系统包括水套缸体，有进出口。此外，水泵壳连接至缸体，水泵吸罩固定至密封水泵壳，并由垫圈加以密封。在垫片的作用下，系统内的水无法从水套溢出，从而达到冷却效果。

**铝壳机体**

水泵壳在冷却系统中驱动水泵套管，起着安装水泵和使其保持恰当位置的重要作用。

**部件购买小窍门**

(1) 要购买新的汽车零部件，禁止使用二手零部件。

(2) 慎重选择供应商，通过推荐、证明和资质证书与供应商建立适当的信任关系。

(3) 对以特别低价提供产品的供应商持谨慎态度。

(4) 订货前，确定从供应商获取产品细节，最好能进行样品检验。

(5) 你需要了解包括与订单相关物资担保与抵押在内的各项条款。

# Unit 10

# ENGINE LUBRICATION SYSTEM
# 发动机润滑系统

【参考视频】

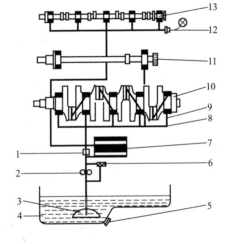

图 10.1  Lubrication system of Santana-2000 type engine
**桑塔纳 2000 型发动机润滑系统**

1—bypass valve 旁通阀；2—oil pump 机油泵；3—oil strainer 集滤器；4—oil bottom housing 油底壳；5—oil drain plug 放油塞；6—safety valve 安全阀；
7—oil filter 机油滤清器；8—primary gallery 主油道；
9—secondary gallery 分油道；10—crank 曲轴；
11—middle crank 中间轴；12—oil pressure switch 油压开关；13—camshaft 凸轮轴

# Unit 10 ENGINE LUBRICATION SYSTEM

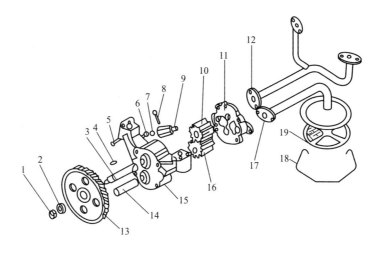

图 10.2  Gear oil pump  齿轮式机油泵

1—nut 螺母；2—key 锁片；3—main drive axle 主动轴；4—woodruff key 半圆键；5—spring seat 弹簧座；6—pressure relief valve spring 限压阀弹簧；7—globe valve 球阀；8—opening pin 开口销；9—valve housing 阀体；10—driving gear 主动齿轮；11—pump cap 泵盖；12—oil outlet pipe 出油管；13—transmission gear 传动齿轮；14—driven axle 从动轴；15—pump housing 泵壳；16—driven gear 从动齿轮；17—drain plug 吸油管；18—cotter 卡簧；19—oil filter net 集滤器滤网

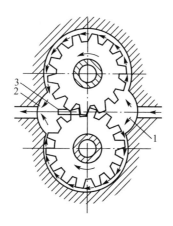

图 10.3  Gear oil pump(schematic) 齿轮式机油泵（示意图）
1—oil inlet body 进油腔；2—oil outlet body 出油腔；
3—unloading pressure baths 卸压槽

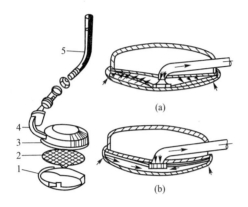

图 10.4  Structure of floating oil filter strainer
浮式集滤器的构造

(a) filter net with lubrication oil passing 润滑油经过滤网
(b) filter net without lubrication oil passing 润滑油不经过滤网
1—cap 罩;  2—filter net 滤网;  3—float 浮子;
4—oil pipe 油管;  5—fixed pipe 固定管

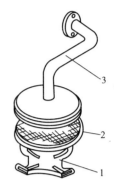

图 10.5  Fixed oil filter strainer
固定式集滤器

1—cap 罩;  2—filter net 滤网;
3—drain plug 吸油管

## Reading Materials

**Passage 1**

### The Lubrication System

The engine lubrication system is designed to deliver clean oil at the correct temperature and pressure to every part of the engine. The oil is sucked out the sump into the pump, being the heart of the system, then forced through an oil filter and pressure feeds to the main bearings and to the oil pressure gauge. From the main bearings, the oil passes through feed-holes into drilled passages in the crankshaft and on to the big-end bearings of the connecting rod. The cylinder walls and piston-pin bearings are lubricated by oil fling dispersed by the rotating crankshaft. The excess is being scraped off by the lower ring in the piston. A bleed or tributary from the main supply passage feeds each camshaft bearing. Another bleed supplies the timing chain or gears on the camshaft drive. The excess oil then drains back to the sump, where the heat is dispersed to the surrounding air.

#### Journal Bearings

If the crankshaft journals become worn the engine will have low oil pressure and throw oil all over the inside of the engine. The excessive splash will probably overwhelm the rings and cause the engine to use oil. Worn bearings surfaces can be restored by simply replacing the bearings inserts. In good maintained engines bearing wear occurs immediately after a cold start, because there's little or no oil film between the bearing and shaft. At the moment that sufficient oil is circulated through the system hydrodynamic lubrication manifests and stops the progress of bearing wear.

### Piston rings—cylinder

Piston rings provide a sliding seal preventing leakage of the fuel-air mixture and exhaust from the combustion chamber into the oil sump during compression and combustion. Secondly they keep oil in the sump from leaking into the combustion area, where it would be burned and lost. Most cars that "burn oil" and have to have a quart added every 1,000 miles are burning it because the rings no longer seal properly.

Between the piston rings and the cylinder wall of a well maintained engine hydrodynamic lubrication prevails, essential for the lowest friction and wear. In the top and bottom dead centre where the piston stops to redirect, the film thickness becomes minimal and mixed lubrication may exist.

To realize a good head transfer from the piston to the cylinder, an optimal sealing and a minimum of oil burning, a minimal film thickness is desirable. The film thickness is kept minimal by a so called oil control ring. This ring is situated beyond the piston rings so that the surplus of oil is directly scraped downwards to the sump. The oil film left on the cylinder wall by the passage of this ring is available to lubricate the following ring. This process is repeated for successive rings. On the up stroke the first compression ring is lubricated by the oil left behind on the cylinder wall during the down stroke.

Leakage of the fuel-air mixture and exhaust from the combustion chamber into the oil sump results in oil degradation. This is the reason why, despite of frequent replenish of oil, oil change remains essential or even becomes more essential.

## 阅读材料

### 材料1（参考译文）

#### 润滑系统

发动机润滑系统的作用是在一定的温度和压力下为发动机各部分提供洁净的机油。机油从储油槽输入主油道（润滑系统的主要组成部分），经由机油滤清器，在压力的作用下进入主轴承和油压力表。在主轴承处，机油经由机油泵入口送入曲轴和连杆的大端轴承，气缸壁和活塞销轴承经旋转曲轴飞溅润滑，多余机油经活塞环刮落。流经主油道的一条支流为凸轮轴轴承提供润滑，另一条支流为凸轮轴驱动定时链或齿轮提供润滑，多余的机油由排油管流回储油槽。储油槽中的热量分散到周围空气中。

#### 轴承

如果曲轴颈发生磨损，则发动机内油压降低，机油会被抛至发动机内部各处。轴瓦和曲轴之间的间隙变大，不能有良好的润滑，且增加油耗。轴承表面磨损更换轴承衬套即可。由于轴承与轴之间的润滑薄膜几乎或者根本不存在，冷起动会直接导致轴承磨损。

当充足的机油在系统循环时,液体动力润滑开始作用,并减少轴承磨损。

**活塞环—气缸**

在压缩和燃烧时,活塞环提供了滑动密封功能,防止燃油-空气混合物和排气从燃烧室进入油底盘。此外,在活塞环的作用下,将阻止机油由油底盘流入燃烧区,在燃烧区机油会进行燃烧。如果活塞环没有密封完好,大多数汽车都会"耗油",平均每1000英里多燃烧1夸脱机油。

保持活塞环和气缸壁的良好润滑必不可少,可将摩擦和磨损降至最低。在活塞活动的顶部和底部中间位置,薄膜厚度降至最小,产生混合润滑。

为了实现活塞和气缸间良好的工作状态,应保持最佳密封,烧机油量降至最低,且实现最小油膜厚度。活塞环可以保证油膜的最小厚度。该环位置超出活塞环,便于剩余的机油被刮到油底盘。有活塞环在气缸壁上留下的油膜可润滑下一个活塞环。这个过程可连续重复实现。上行行程的第一个压缩环通过气缸壁左侧机油在下行行程时润滑。

来自燃烧室的燃油空气混合物和废气残留部分进入机油箱,将导致机油降级。因此,即使经常加油,也要经常更换机油。

## Passage 2

### How the Lubrication System Works

Lubrication is employed to reduce friction by interposing a film between rubbing parts. The lubrication system must continuously replace the film. The lubricants commonly employed are refined from crude oil after the fuels have been removed. Their viscosities must be appropriate for each engine, and the oil must be suitable for the severity of the operating conditions. Oils are improved with additives that reduce oxidation, inhibit corrosion, and act as detergents to disperse deposit-forming gums and solid contaminants. Motor oils also include an antifoaming agent. Various systems of numbers are used to designate oil viscosity; the lower the number, the lighter the body of the oil. Viscosity must be chosen to match the flow rate of oil through a part to the designed cooling requirements of the part. If the oil is too thick it will not flow through the part fast enough to properly dissipate heat. Certain oils contain additives that oppose their change in viscosity between winter and summer.

Oil filters, if regularly serviced, can remove solid contaminants from crankcase oil, but chemical reactions may form liquids that are corrosive and damaging. Depletion of the additives also limits the useful life of lubricating oils.

The lubrication system is fed by the oil sump that forms the lower enclosure of the engine. Oil is taken from the sump by a pump, usually of the gear type, and is passed through a filter and delivered under pressure to a system of passages or channels drilled through the engine. Virtually all modern engines use full-flow type oil filters. Filtered oil is supplied under pressure to crankshaft and camshaft main bearings. Adjacent crank

## Unit 10  ENGINE LUBRICATION SYSTEM

throws are drilled to enable the oil to flow from the supply at the main bearings to the crank pins. Leaking oil from all of the crankshaft bearings is sprayed on the cylinder walls, cams, and up into the pistons to lubricate the piston pins. Additional passages intersect the cam-follower openings and supply oil to hydraulic valve lifters when used. A spring-loaded pressure-relief valve maintains the pressure at the proper level. Oil is important for both lubrication and cooling.

### 材料2 (参考译文)

#### 润滑系统的工作原理

润滑的作用是通过薄膜减少摩擦部件之间的摩擦。润滑系统必须不断更换油膜。常用润滑油是将原油提炼燃料后再提炼所得的。其黏度必须适合所有发动机,必须满足机油运转所需。机油添加剂可减少氧化,抑制腐蚀,作为清洁剂清洁长期形成的污垢和固体污染物。车用机油中包含消泡剂。数字系统用来指定机油黏度:数值越低,油体越轻。选择的机油黏度必须与机油流量的冷却设计要求相匹配。如果机油过厚,影响流速,不能有效散热。有些机油含有添加剂,冬夏两季由于天气过热或过冷对黏度产生影响。

机油滤清器,如果定期加以保养,可以从曲轴箱有效去除固体污染物,但其中产生的化学反应可能形成具有腐蚀性和破坏性的液体。添加剂的消耗也缩短了润滑油的使用寿命。

润滑系由发动机下端的油底盘供给。机油从油底盘经集滤器被机油泵送入机油滤清器。现代发动机几乎都使用全流式机油滤清器。过滤机油通过压力进入曲轴主轴承和凸轮轴。相邻的曲柄弯程使机油由曲轴箱流向主轴承。曲轴轴承漏油飞溅至气缸壁、凸轮以及活塞销。额外的油道横断凸轮从动口及供油液压起阀器。弹簧加载降压阀保持适当水平的压力。机油对润滑和冷却都尤为重要。

# Unit 11

# ENGINE STARTING SYSTEM
# 发动机起动系统

【参考视频】

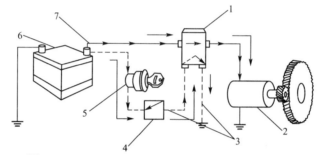

图 11.1  Starting systems components  起动系统组成
1—electromagnetic switch 电磁开关；2—starter 起动机；3—control circuit 控制电路；4—starter relay 起动机继电器；5—ignition switch 点火开关；6—battery 蓄电池；7—starter circuit 起动机电路

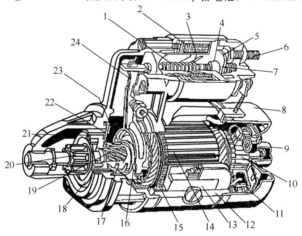

图 11.2  Starter assembly  起动机总成
1—reset spring 复位弹簧；2、3—electromagnetic switch 电磁开关；4—moveable contact 动触点；5—moveable contact disc 活动触盘；6—battery connector 蓄电池接线柱；7—contact 触点；8—front cover 前端盖；9—brush spring 电刷弹簧；10—commutator 换向器；11—brush 电刷；12—housing 机壳；13—magnet pole 磁极；14—armature 电枢；15—magnetic field winding 磁场绕组；16—guide ring 导向环；17—anti-thrust ring 止推环；18—one-way clutch 单向离合器；19—armature shaft 电枢轴；20—drive gear 驱动齿轮；21—transmission 传动机构；22—braking disk 制动盘；23—meshing spring 啮合弹簧；24—fork 拨叉

## Unit 11  ENGINE STARTING SYSTEM

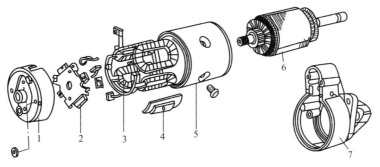

图 11.3  Direct current motor  直流电动机

1—cover 端盖；2—brush and case 电刷和电刷架；3—magnetic field winding 磁场绕组；
4—magnet pole core 磁极铁心；5—housing 机壳；6—armature 电枢；7—back cover 后端盖

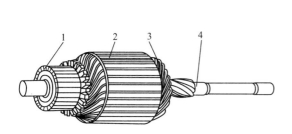

图 11.4  Armature assembly  电枢总成

1—commutator 换向器；2—core 铁心；
3—winding 绕组；4—armature shaft 电枢轴

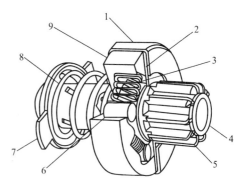

图 11.5  One-way clutch  单向离合器的结构

1—housing 外壳；2—ball plate 滚珠挡板；
3—ball spring 滚珠弹簧；4—brass bush 铜套；
5—drive gear 驱动齿轮；6—ball 滚珠；
7—pushing flange 推动凸缘；8—cusion
spring 缓冲弹簧；9—clutch outer ring
离合器外环

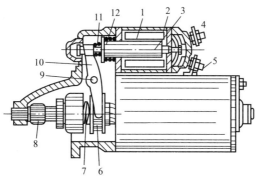

图 11.6  Electromagnetic fork  电磁式拨叉

1—coil 线圈；2—housing 外壳；3—electromagnet core 电磁铁心；4、5—connection bolt 接线柱；
6—fork 拨叉；7—cusion spring 缓冲弹簧；8—drive gear 驱动齿轮；9—fork axis 拨叉轴；
10—fork 拨叉；11、12—spring 弹簧

## Reading Materials

Passage 1

### The Starting System

The automobile engines are self-starting equipment. In order to start them, the starting system is designed to turn or "crank" the engine until it can operate under its own power. To do this, the starter motor receives electrical power from the storage battery. The starter motor then converts electrical energy into mechanical energy, which transmits through the drive mechanism to the engines flywheel.

A typical starting system has five basic components and two distinct electrical circuits. The components are:

(1) Battery;

(2) Ignition switch;

(3) Battery cables;

(4) Starting relay;

(5) Starter motor.

The starter motor draws a great deal of electrical current from the battery. A large starter motor might require 300 to 400 amperes of current. This current flows through the heavy cables that connect the battery to the starter.

The driver controls the flow of this current using the starting switch. However, if the cables was routed from the battery to the starting switch and then on to the starter motor, the voltage drop caused by resistance in the cables would be too great. To avoid this problem, the system is designed with two connected circuits: the starter circuit and the control circuit.

The starter circuit carries the high current flow within the system and supplies power for the actual engine cranking. Components of the starter circuit are the battery, battery cables, ignition switch or starting relay and the starter motor.

### Starting Safety Switch

The starting safety switch is also called a neutral starting switch. It is a normally open switch that prevents the starting systems from operating when the automobile's transmission is in gear. If the car has no starting safety switch, it is possible to pin the engine with the transmission in gear. This will make the car lurch forward or backward which could be dangerous. The safety switch can be an electrical switch that opens the control circuit if the car is in gear. It can also be a mechanical interlock device that will not let the ignition switch turn to start if the car is in gear.

### Magnetic Switch

A magnetic switch in the starting system allows the control circuit to open and close

# Unit 11  ENGINE STARTING SYSTEM

the starter circuit. The switch can be a:

(1) Relay which uses the electromagnetic field of a coil to attract an armature and close the contact points.

(2) Solenoid which uses the electromagnetic field of a coil to pull a plunger into the coil and close the contact points. The plunger's movement can also be used to do a mechanical job.

### Starter Motor

The starter motor converts electrical energy from the battery into mechanical energy to turn the engine. It does this through the interaction of magnetic fields when current flow through a conductor, a magnetic field is formed around the conductor. If the conductor is placed in another magnetic field, the two fields will be weakened at one side and strengthened at the other side. The conductor will tend to move from the strong field into the weak field, showing how a simple motor can use this movement to make the conductor rotate. An automotive starter motor has many conductors and uses a lot of current to create enough rotational force to crank the engine.

 阅读材料

**材料1（参考译文）**

## 起 动 系 统

汽车发动机是自起动装置。为了起动发动机，设计了起动系统，由它带动发动机运转直到发动机可以自行运转。为实现这一点，起动机先接受来自蓄电池的电能，再把电能转化成机械能，再将机械能通过传动装置传给发动机飞轮。

一个典型的起动系统有五个基本组成部分和两个不同的电路。这五个组成部分分别是：

（1）蓄电池；

（2）点火开关；

（3）蓄电池电缆；

（4）起动继电器；

（5）起动机。

蓄电池向起动机提供的电流很大。一个大的起动机可能需要300～400安的电流。电流通过连接在蓄电池和起动机之间的较粗的电缆送到起动机里。

驾驶员通过点火开关来控制这个电流。但是，如果电路的连接方式是从蓄电池到点火开关再到起动机，由于电缆电阻造成的电压下降会太大。为了避免这个问题，该系统设计了两个连接电路：起动电路和控制电路。

起动电路向系统内提供大电流并为发动机起动提供能量。起动电路包括蓄电池、蓄电池电缆、点火开关、起动继电器和起动机。

### 起动安全开关

起动安全开关又称空挡起动开关。这是一个常开开关,防止起动系统在汽车变速器挂上挡的时候工作。如果汽车没有起动安全开关,它可能在汽车变速器挂上挡的时候使起动机带动发动机运转,这将使汽车蹒跚向前或向后,很危险。当汽车挂上挡后,该安全开关是一个电子开关,它会自动断开控制电路。它也是机械连锁装置,如果汽车挂上挡,它不会让点火开关转到起动位置。

### 电磁开关

起动系统中的电磁开关允许控制电路打开和关闭起动电路。该开关可以是一个:

(1)继电器:利用线圈的电磁场来吸引电枢并闭合触点。

(2)电磁线圈:利用线圈的电磁场把一个柱塞拉进线圈中并且闭合触点,柱塞的运动也可以用来做机械工作。

### 起动机

起动机把蓄电池的电能转换成驱动发动机运转的机械能,它是通过磁场的相互作用来实现的。当电流通过一个导体,导体的周围就会生成一个磁场。如果导体被放置在另一个磁场中,这个磁场会将一边被削弱,另一边得到加强。导体往往会从强的磁场移动到弱磁场,这就展示了一个简单的起动机是如何利用这种运动使导体旋转的。一个汽车起动机里有许多导体,并且利用大量的电流来产生足够的旋转力来带动发动机运转。

Passage 2

#### When to Replace Your Automobile Starter Motor

If you try to start your vehicle and the engine turns too slowly, or not at all, the starter or starter solenoid may need to be replaced. Before you go through the steps of replacing parts always do a few trouble shooting detection to make sure that starter or the solenoid is the problem. Because the starter and the solenoid work together its always best to replace them together.

Starter motor trouble shooting tips:

(1) Check the battery cables and terminals if needed.

(2) Clean the corrosion and replace the battery or cables if needed.

(3) Check the wires to the starter and the solenoid for cracks, corrosion, or breakage.

Make sure your battery is charged enough to perform starting functions. Note: your instrument lights and dome lights may come on but your battery may still not have enough power to start the car.

Remember electrical parts fail mostly in part to time and usage not because of wear and tear like mechanical parts. And the damage is mostly in the internal electrical wiring, so some failures can not be noticed from an outside inspection. If you have done the tests

## Unit 11  ENGINE STARTING SYSTEM

listed above and are still having problems starting your vehicle, then here are the steps to follow for proper installation of your automobile's starter motor.

Starter motor installation steps:

Gather the necessary tools needed such as wrenches, sockets, screwdriver and pliers.

(1) Place the vehicle on ramps or jack up the front and support with jack stands. It is very important to block the rear wheels to keep the car stationary during this procedure. Never work under a vehicle not supported properly.

(2) Make sure ignition is off and the remove the negative battery cable from the battery.

(3) Note the location of all wires before removal to make for easier connection.

(4) Remove the large starter cable going to the battery at the starter location.

(5) Remove any other wires attached to the solenoid.

(6) Remove the starter attaching bolts.

(7) Remove any supporting brackets that hold the starter.

(8) Drop the starter down away from the car.

(9) Install the new starter in the reverse order of removal.

(10) Reconnect battery cables and other wires to solenoid.

(11) Place old starter in the new starter box for proper core return.

If you have followed these simple steps then you should have a new automobile starter motor installed on your vehicle for free starting.

## 材料2（参考译文）

### 什么时候更换汽车发动机

如果你打算起动车辆而发动机转得太慢或根本不转，那么可能是起动机或起动机电磁线圈需要更换。在更换零件前，应做一些故障排除检测，以确保起动机或电磁线圈有问题。由于电动机和电磁线圈共同工作，所以最好二者一起更换。

起动机故障排除技巧：

(1) 检查蓄电池和端子。

(2) 清洁腐蚀物，更换蓄电池或电缆。

(3) 检查起动机和电磁线圈的导线是否有裂缝、腐蚀或破损。

确保蓄电池有足够的电来起动发动机。注意：有时仪表灯和顶灯依然亮着，但是蓄电池可能已经没有足够的电来起动汽车了。

记住电子零件大部分会由于时间和使用而失效，而不像机械零件会由于磨损而失效，并且损坏主要是在内部的电路，因此有些故障外部检查发现不了。如果你做了上述的检查，起动车辆的时候仍然有问题，你可以按照下面的步骤来正确安装汽车起动机。

起动机安装步骤：

准备好必要的工具，如扳手、插座、螺钉旋具和钳子。

（1）把车辆放置在斜坡上或者用千斤顶顶起前部并用支撑架支撑住。此过程中挡住后轮并保持车辆静止是非常重要的，坚决不要在没有支撑好的车辆下面工作。

（2）确保点火开关是关闭的并且把蓄电池负极的电缆线拆下。

（3）注意所有电缆拆去前的位置，以使连接更容易。

（4）拆去起动机到蓄电池的较粗的电缆线。

（5）拆去和电磁线圈相连的任何导线。

（6）拆去起动机的固定螺栓。

（7）拆除所有支撑起动机的托架。

（8）把起动机从汽车上拆下来。

（9）按照和拆卸相反的顺序把一个新的起动机安装在车辆上。

（10）把蓄电池电缆和电磁线圈相连的导线重新连接起来。

（11）将旧的起动机放在新的起动机盒子里以备回收。

如果遵循这些简单的步骤，那么你的汽车有了一个新的起动机，并且起动应该也相当轻松。

# Unit 12

# AUTOMOBILE POWER TRAIN
# 汽车传动系统

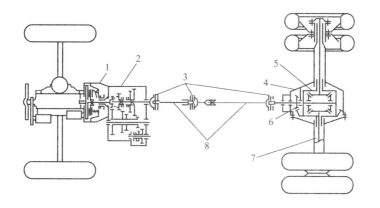

图 12.1　Power train　传动系
1—clutch 离合器；2—transmission 变速器；3—universal joint 万向节；
4—driving axle 驱动桥；5—differential 差速器；6—final drive
主减速器；7—axle shaft 半轴；8—drive shaft 传动轴

【参考视频】

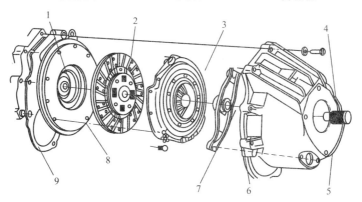

图 12.2　Clutch assembly　离合器总成
1—pilot bearing 导向轴承；2—clutch friction lining 离合器摩擦片；3—pressure and cover
压盘与罩；4—input shaft 输入轴；5—clutch housing 离合器壳；
6—release lever 分离杆；7—release bearing 分离轴承；
8—flywheel 飞轮；9—cover plate 罩板

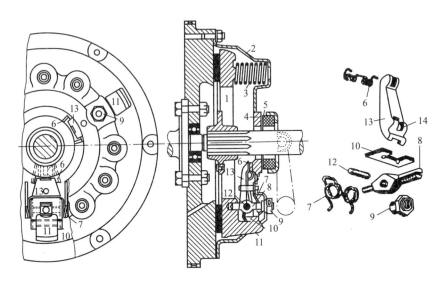

图 12.3 Coil spring clutch 螺旋弹簧式离合器

1—pressure plate 压盘；2—clutch cover 离合器盖；3—pressure spring 压紧弹簧；4—annular plate 环形板；5—carbon-impregnated ring 渗碳环；6—retained spring 保持弹簧；7—release lever spring 分离杆弹簧；8—eye bolt 环首螺栓；9—adjusting nut 调节螺母；10—strut 支撑片；11—pressure plate lug 压盘凸耳；12—pivot 枢销；13—release lever 分离杠杆；14—recess 凹座

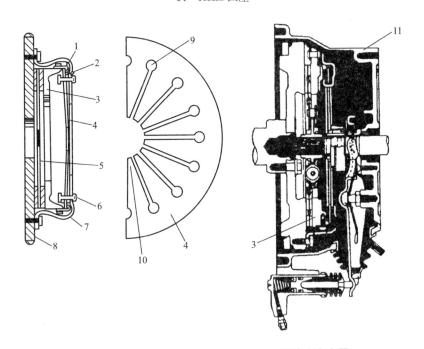

图 12.4 Diaphragm spring clutch 膜片弹簧式离合器

1—return spring 回位弹簧；2—pivot ring 支枢环；3—pressure plate 压盘；4—diaphragm spring 膜片弹簧；5—driven plate 从动盘；6—returning bolt(支枢环)固定螺栓；7—clutch cover 离合器盖；8—flywheel 飞轮；9—blunted location hole 圆形定位孔；10—diaphragm release finger 膜片分离指；11—clutch housing 离合器壳

# Unit 12　AUTOMOBILE POWER TRAIN

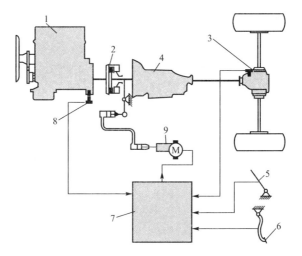

图 12.5　Automatic transmission　自动离合器

1—engine 发动机；2—clutch 离合器；3—vehicle-speed sensor 车速传感器；
4—transmission 变速器；5—accelerator 加速踏板；6—clutch pedal
离合器踏板；7—control unit 控制模块；8—engine-speed sensor
发动机转速传感器；9—servo motor 伺服电动机

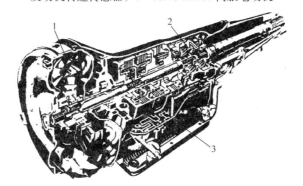

图 12.6　Three basic systems of automatic transmission　自动变速器的三个基本系统

1—torque converter 液力变矩器；2—gear system 齿轮系统；
3—hydraulic system 液压系统

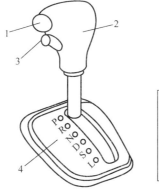

挡位缩写
P=parking 驻车挡
R=reverse 倒挡
N=neutral 空挡
D=driving 前进挡
S=second 第二挡
L=low 低挡

图 12.7　Selector lever of automatic transmission　自动变速器变速杆

1—shaft lock button 锁止按钮；2—shift lever 变速杆；3—O/D switch(overdrive switch)超速挡开关；4—shift position indicator 挡位指示器

【参考视频】

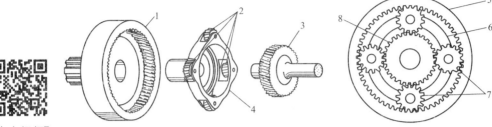

图12.8 The simple planetary gear system 行星齿轮机构

1、5—ring gear 齿圈；2、7—planet gear 行星轮；3、8—sun gear 太阳轮；4、6—planet carrier 行星架

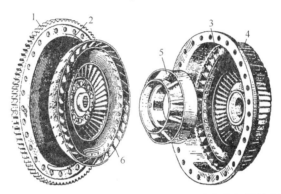

图12.9 Main parts of the Torque converter 液力变矩器的主要零件

1—start up ring gear 起动齿圈；2—converter cover 变矩器壳；3—impeller 泵轮；4—converter cover 变矩器壳；5—stator 导轮；6—turbine 涡轮

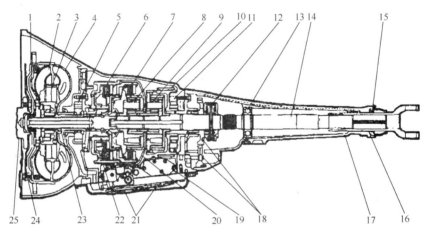

图12.10 Cross-sectional view of typical automatic transmission 典型自动变速器的剖视图

1—lock-up clutch 锁止离合器；2—turbine 涡轮；3—stator 导轮；4—impeller 泵轮；5—oil pump 油泵；6—front clutch 前离合器；7—rear clutch 后离合器；8—front planetary gear set 前行星齿轮组；9—rear planetary gear set 后行星齿轮组；10—low and reverse band 低、倒挡制动带；11—overrunning clutch 超越离合器；12—governor 调速器；13—bearing 轴承；14—output shaft 输出轴；15—seal 油封；16—bushing 套管；17—extension housing 加长壳体；18—parking lock assembly 驻车锁总成；19—valve body 阀体；20—sun gear driving shell 太阳轮驱动壳体；21—oil filter 机油滤清器；22—kick down band 强制降挡制动带；23—input shaft 输入轴；24—flexible drive plate 挠性驱动盘；25—engine crankshaft 发动机曲轴

## Unit 12　AUTOMOBILE POWER TRAIN

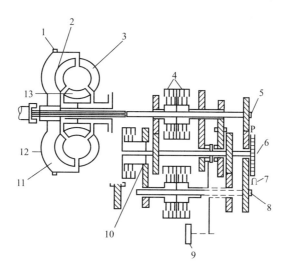

图 12.11　Automatic transmission　自动变速器

1—start up ring gear 起动齿圈；2—turbine 涡轮；3—stator 导轮；4—clutch 离合器；
5—input shaft 输入轴；6—countershaft 中间轴；7—parking lock 停车锁；
8—output shaft 输出轴；9—servo value 伺服阀；10—one-way clutch
单向离合器；11—converter 变矩器；12—converter cover
变矩器壳；13—impeller 泵轮

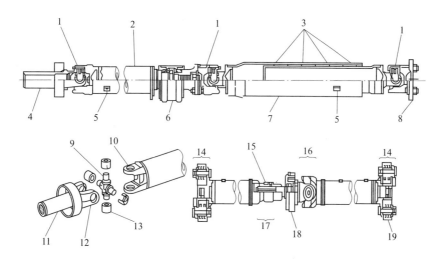

图 12.12　Drive shaft　传动轴

1—universal joint 万向节；2—countershaft 中间轴；3—rubber absorber 橡胶减振器；4—sleeve
yoke 套筒叉；5—balance weight 平衡重；6—center support 中间支撑；7—drive shaft 传动轴；
8—flange yoke 凸缘叉；9—cross spider 十字轴；10—weld yoke/tube yoke 万向节叉；
11—sleeve yoke 套筒叉；12—weld yoke/tube yoke 万向节叉；13—round universal
joint 挠性万向节；14—flexible universal joint 挠性万向节；15—adjusting nut
调整螺母；16—universal joint 万向节；17—adjusting nut 调整螺母；
18—center support 中间支撑；19—flexible coupling 挠性万向节

97

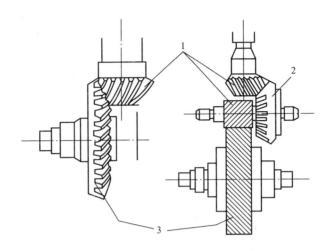

图 12.13　Final drive　主减速器

1—drive pinion 主动齿轮；2、3—driven pinion 从动齿轮

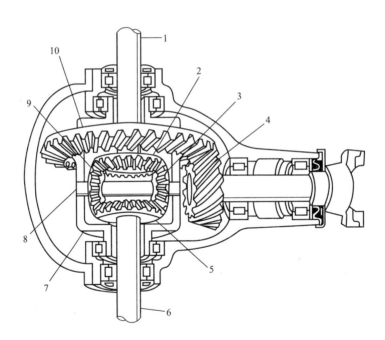

图 12.14　Different　差速器

1、6—axle shaft 半轴；2—side gear 半轴齿轮；3、9—differential pinion 差速器小齿轮；4—drive pinion 主动小齿轮；5—side gear 半轴齿轮；7—differential case 差速器壳；8—pinion shaft 小齿轮轴；10—ring gear 齿圈

Unit 12　AUTOMOBILE POWER TRAIN

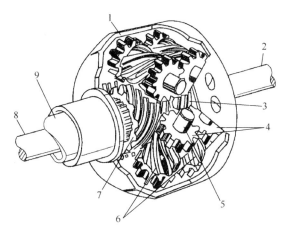

图 12.15　Torsen differential　托森差速器

1—differential case 差速器壳；2—differential rear gear shaft 差速器后齿轮轴；
3—rear shaft worm 后轴蜗杆；4—spur gear 直齿圆柱齿轮；5—turbine shaft
涡轮轴；6—turbine 涡轮；7—front shaft worm 前轴蜗杆；8—differential
front gear shaft 差速器前齿轮轴；9—hollow shaft 空心轴

## Reading Materials

### Passage 1

#### Automobile Power Train

The power developed inside the engine cylinder is ultimately aimed to turn the wheels so that the motor vehicle can move on the road. The reciprocating motion of the piston turns a crankshaft rotating the flywheel through the connecting rod. The circular motion of the crankshaft is now to be transmitted to the driving wheels. It is transmitted through the clutch on manual transmission or torque converter on automatic transmission, a transmission, universal joints, propeller shaft or drive shaft, final drive, differential and half shaft extending to the wheels. The application of engine power to the driving wheels through all these parts is called power train. The power train is usually the same on all modern passenger cars and trucks, but its arrangement may vary according to the method of drive and type of transmission units.

The power train serves two functions: it transmits power from the engine to the drive wheels, and it varies the amount of torque. The power train includes:

(1) Clutch: used only on manual transmission; or torque converter: used only on automatic transmission;

(2) Transmission: either manual or automatic;

(3) Universal joint: that permits movement between the final drive and transmission;

(4) Drive shaft: that transmits the power from transmission to differential;

(5) Final drive: that turns the drive through 90° and reduces the speed of the drive;

(6) Differential: that carries the power to the two wheel axles;

(7) Axle shaft: that carries the power to the two wheels.

**Power Train Components**

### Clutch

The clutch is a device used to provide smooth engagement and disengagement of engine and transmission. The engagement of engine and transmission means the link-up between engine and power train to transfer the engine power to the driving axle and wheels, and their disengagement means the halt to power transfer that allows the engine to operate while the transmission does not. Three types of clutch are coil spring type, diaphragm spring type and semi-centrifugal type.

In conjunction with electronic control unit, automatic clutches provide automatic drive away, or, together with servo-operated manual transmission, they provide a fully automatic transmission. Electronic traction control as well as power interruption during braking are likewise possible.

### Transmission

There are two types of transmission—manual transmission (MT) and automatic transmission (AT). In a car with a manual transmission, a driver shifts the gears manually. In a car with an automatic transmission, the gears shift automatically.

A manual transmission requires use of a clutch to apply and remove engine torque to the transmission input shaft. The clutch allows this to happen gradually so that the car can be started from a complete stop.

Manual transmissions usually have four or five speeds, and often have "overdrive", which means that the output shaft can turn faster than the input shaft for fuel economy on the highway. When you use it, it will reduce the engine speed by one-third, while maintaining the same road speed.

An automatic transmission is a device that provides gear reduction, with resulting multiplication of torque. The gear ranges are automatically selected to provide the most efficient operation and the best torque output.

Automatic transmission have three basic systems—a torque converter, a gear system and a hydraulic system.

The gear system changes the ratio in the automatic transmission. The planetary gear system has three parts—the sun gear, the planet gears and carrier, and the internal gear or ring gear.

The torque converter is like the clutch in a manual transmission. It is the coupling between the engine and power train that transmits power to the drive wheels.

It has three parts that help multiply the power: an impeller(or pump)connected to the engine's crankshaft, a turbine to turn the turbine shaft which is connected to the gears, and a stator(or guide wheel) between the two.

### Universal joint

A universal joint is used where two shafts are connected at an angle to transmit torque. In the transmission system of a motor vehicle, the transmission main shaft, propeller shaft and the final drive pinion shaft are not in one line, and hence the connections between them are made by universal joint. One universal joint is used to connect the transmission main shaft and the propeller shaft, the other universal joint is used to connect the other end of the propeller shaft and the final drive pinion shaft. Thus, the connections between the three shafts are flexible and at an angle with each other. The universal joint permits the torque transmission not only at angle, but also while this angle is changing constantly.

### Drive shaft

The drive shaft transmits the drive from the transmission mainshaft to the final drive pinion shaft. The drive shaft is not solidly bolted to the transmission and the final drive. There must be some allowance for motion between the final drive and transmission. The universal joints provide this coupling.

### Final drive

The final drive transfers power from the engine and transmission to the wheels that drive the car. The final drive takes power from the spinning drive shaft and transfers it 90° to make the drive wheels turn. The final drive assembly also provides gear reduction so that the drive wheel spin more slowly than the drive shaft. The gear reduction varies depending on engine size and power, engine torque, and vehicle size and weight.

The final drive works fine as long as both drive wheels turn at the speed. However, this system cannot provide different rates of speed for different wheels. A differential system is needed to allow for speed differences. This gear system is the heart of the final drive assembly.

### Differential

When a car moves straight ahead, the drive wheels have an equal amount of traction. When a car goes around a corner, power can no longer be divided evenly between the two side gears.

When it reaches the differential pinion, as a result, the outside wheel turns faster than the inside wheel.

Torsen differential is a new pattern differential mechanism, and is used on FWD vehicle widely. Audi 80 and Audi 90(Audi Quattro) full wheel drive saloon car adopt this new pattern Torsen differential between front axle and rear axle.

**Axle shaft**

The axle shaft(half shaft)connects the differential sun wheel to the road wheel.

 阅读材料

材料1（参考译文）

## 汽车传动系统

发动机气缸内的能量最终是用来驱动车轮运动的，以使车辆能在道路上行驶。活塞的往复运动通过连杆带动曲轴旋转，曲轴再带动飞轮旋转，曲轴的圆周运动就传到了驱动轮上。能量传递路径为：离合器（如果是手动变速器）或液力变矩器（如果是自动变速器）、变速器、万向节、传动轴、主减速器、差速器、和车轮相连的半轴。把发动机的能量传递到车轮上的所有部件所组成的系统称为传动系。所有现代乘用车和货车上的传动系统通常是相同的，但根据驱动方式和变速器种类的不同，传动系统的布置可能有所不同。

传动系统有两个功能：把发动机的动力传递到驱动轮并改变发动机发出的转矩。传动系统包括：

(1) 离合器（仅在手动变速器）或液力变矩器（只用于自动变速器）。

(2) 变速器：手动或自动的。

(3) 万向节：使主减速器和变速器之间可以有相对运动。

(4) 传动轴：把动力从变速器传到差速器。

(5) 主减速器：把发动机动力传递方向改变90°并且降低发动机的转速。

(6) 差速器：把动力传递到两个半轴上。

(7) 半轴：把动力传递到两个车轮上。

### 传动系统组成

#### 离合器

离合器是用于使发动机和变速器之间平稳接合和脱离的装置。发动机和变速器的接合意味着发动机和传动系连接到一起，把发动机的能量传送到驱动轴和驱动轮；其脱离意味着发动机动力传递的停止，发动机运转而变速器不工作。离合器有三种类型：螺旋弹簧式、膜片弹簧式和半离心式。

自动离合器与电子控制单元相结合，可以自动起步，或者和伺服操作手动变速器一起，可以提供一个完全自动变速器，也可以实现电子牵引力控制以及制动时的动力中断。

#### 变速器

变速器有两种类型：手动变速器（MT）与自动变速器（AT）。在手动变速器汽车上，驾驶者手动地换挡；在自动变速器汽车上，挡位可以自动切换。

手动变速器需要用一个离合器来把发动机的转矩传递给变速器输入轴或从变速器的

输入轴上断开。离合器可以使发动机和变速器柔和地接合与分离，从而使汽车可以从完全静止起步。

手动变速器，通常有4或5个挡位，而且通常有"超速挡"，这意味着在高速公路上，为了燃油经济性可以使输出轴比输入轴旋转得快。当使用超速挡的时候，它可以在保持相同的车速的情况下把发动机转速降低到原来的1/3。

自动变速器是一种减速增扭的装置。挡位可以自动选择以提供最有效的运作和最佳的转矩输出。

自动变速器有三个基本系统：液力变矩器、齿轮系统和液压系统。

齿轮系统改变自动变速器的传动比。行星齿轮系统由三部分组成：太阳轮、行星轮和行星架、内齿轮或齿圈。

液力变矩器像是手动变速器的离合器。它是发动机和传动系之间的连接器，把动力传递到驱动轮。

液力变矩器由三部分组成，以利于扩大动力：和发动机曲轴相连的叶轮（或泵轮）；和齿轮连接用来带动涡轮轴旋转的涡轮；位于泵轮和涡轮之间的定子（或导轮）。

### 万向节

万向节用以传递以一定角度相连接的两个轴之间的动力。在汽车的传动系统中，变速器输出轴、传动轴和主减速器输入轴不在一条直线上，因此它们之间用万向节来连接。一个万向节被用来连接变速器输出轴和传动轴，另外一个万向节是用来连接传动轴的另一端和主减速器的输入轴。这样，这三个轴之间的连接是柔性的并且彼此互成一定角度。万向节不仅使转矩的传递成一定角度，而且这个角度是不断变化的。

### 传动轴

传动轴把动力从变速器输出轴传递到主减速器输入轴。传动轴不是用螺栓把变速器和主减速器刚性地连接到一起，它允许变速器和主减速器的相对运动，万向节提供了这种连接。

### 主减速器

主减速器把动力从发动机和变速器传送到车轮，驱动汽车运动。主减速器从旋转的传动轴获得动力，并把动力传动方向改变90度驱动驱动轮旋转。主减速器总成也有降挡功能，以使驱动轮比传动轴旋转得慢。降挡的范围取决于发动机的尺寸和功率、发动机转矩、车辆尺寸和质量。

只要两驱动轮的速度相同，主减速器就能工作正常。然而，该系统不能使不同的车轮以不同的速度转动。所以就需要有一个差速器来实现不同的轮速。齿轮系统是主减速器总成的核心部件。

### 差速器

当汽车直线前进的时候，驱动轮上牵引力是相等的。当汽车转弯的时候，动力不再平均分配给两半轴齿轮。

当动力到达差速器小齿轮的时候，产生的结果是外面的齿轮比里面的齿轮旋转得快。

托森差速器是一种新型差速器,用在全轮驱动的车辆上。奥迪80和奥迪90(奥迪Quattro)全轮驱动轿车在前桥和后桥之间采用了这种新型的托森差速器。

### 半轴

半轴用来连接差速器太阳轮和车轮。

## Passage 2

### Industry Overview

Along with the increase in automatic transmission cars, China's development prospects of the traditional clutch industry growing concern, many companies are seeking new ways of sustainable development. Prior to 2007, China's vehicle production continued to grow, the increase in car ownership and export market demand, the three major factors promote the development of China's automotive clutch industry for 8 consecutive years rapidly. In 2007 China's output of clutch broke 10 million units. Since 2008, the global financial crisis, China's vehicle sales to 9.38 million, only 6.7% growth rate, the market size of clutch is about 5.5 billion. 2010 China's auto market would bottom out, then the clutch total sales will be expected to exceed 8 billion yuan.

DCT technology's good prospects in China, will bring new development opportunities to China friction plate clutch industry. However, the market competition is fierce, Changchun Yidong Clutch which is the leader of domestic auto clutch manufacturing industry, has formed the productivity of 750,000 sets. It is the largest clutch manufacturer and has the widest series of clutches, which enjoys high industry status. The company is in the leading position in the OE market. It is the supplier of 64 factories, occupying the domestic medium and heavy commercial vehicle market in half.

Dual mass flywheel clutch is a traditional development trend. Our country has Luk, Excedy and other foreign companies in China, assembling dual-mass flywheel, Jilin Da hua, Hubei Tri-ring of the double mass flywheel also entered the industrialization stage, but dual mass flywheel development prospects in China are still subject to further market validation.

The demand of torque converter is increasing along with the increase of the proportion of China's auto automatic transmission. In domestic market, Shanghai Sachs had torque converter products long ago. Guangzhou Youdajia, Shanghai Excedy, Nanjing Valeo and other foreign companies already have begun to assemble torque converter. Since the localization of AT technology is very difficult, developing torque converter for the domestic enterprises still has higher risk.

**材料 2（参考译文）**

## 行业概览

随着我国自动挡轿车的增加，我国传统离合器行业的发展前景日益堪忧，不少企业都在寻求新的持续发展的途径。2007年以前，我国汽车产量持续增长、汽车保有量的增加、出口市场需求的扩张三大因素推动了我国汽车离合器行业连续8年快速发展。2007年我国汽车离合器的产量突破1 000万套。自2008年以来，受全球金融危机影响，中国汽车销量为938万辆，增长率仅为6.7%，离合器的市场规模约为55亿元。预计到2010年，中国车市将走出低谷，届时离合器总销售额将有望突破80亿元。

DCT技术在中国有良好的发展前景，这将使我国摩擦片汽车离合器行业获得新的发展机遇。但是，市场竞争也很激烈，长春一东离合器股份有限公司是国内汽车离合器制造行业龙头企业，已形成75万套的生产力，是国内规模最大，系列最全的离合器生产厂家，行业地位较高。公司在主机配套市场处于龙头地位，面向全国64家主机厂供货，占领了国内中重型商用车市场的半壁江山。

双质量飞轮是我国传统汽车离合器发展的一种方向，目前我国已经有Luk，Excedy等外资企业在中国组装生产双质量飞轮，吉林大华、湖北三环的双质量飞轮也进入产业化阶段，但双质量飞轮在我国发展前景依然有待市场进一步验证。

液力变矩器需求随着我国自动挡汽车比重的增加而加大，国内除上海萨克斯早已量产液力变矩器产品外，广州优达佳、上海Excedy、南京Valeo等外资企业已经相继开始组装生产液力变矩器。由于我国AT技术的本土化存在很大困难，发展液力变矩器对国内企业仍存在较高的风险。

# Unit 13

# AUTOMOBILE RUNNING GEAR
# 汽车行驶系统

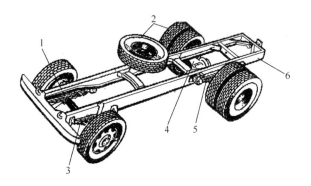

图 13.1　Running gear　行驶系统
1—front axle 前桥；2—wheel 车轮；3—front suspension 前悬架；4—rear axle 后桥；5—rear suspension 后悬架；6—frame 车架

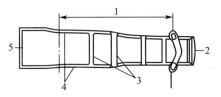

图 13.2　Simple frame　简单的车架
1—wheel base 轮距；2—front 前端；3—cross members 横梁；4—side members 纵梁；5—rear 后端

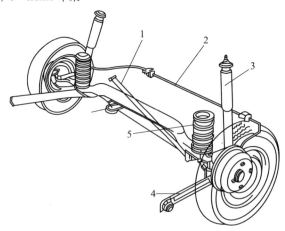

图 13.3　Suspension assembly　悬架总成
1—transverse tie rod 横向推力杆；2—transverse stabilizer 横向稳定器；3—shock absorber 减振器；4—longitudinal rod 纵向推力杆；5—spring element 弹性元件

Unit 13　AUTOMOBILE RUNNING GEAR

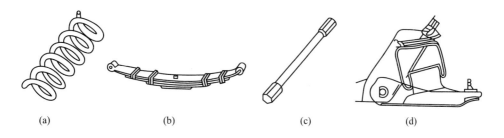

图 13.4　Four basic types of springs　弹簧的四种基本类型
(a) coil spring 螺旋弹簧；(b) leaf spring 钢板弹簧；(c) torsion bar spring 扭杆弹簧；
(d) air spring 空气弹簧

图 13.5　Leaf spring assembly　钢板弹簧总成
1—center bolt 中心螺栓；2—main leaf 主片；
3—rebound clip 缓冲夹；4—spring eye 弹簧卷耳

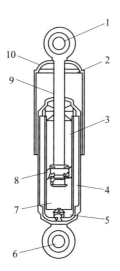

图 13.6　The inside parts of a shock absorber　减振器内部部件
1—upper mounting 上支撑；2—rod guide 连杆导向座；3—rebound chamber
回弹室；4—reserve chamber 储油室；5—compression intake valve 压缩阀；
6—lower mounting 下支撑；7—compression chamber 压缩室；
8—piston and rebound valve 活塞和伸张阀；9—piston
rod 活塞杆；10—adhesive sealant 密封胶

汽车专业英语图解教程（第 2 版）

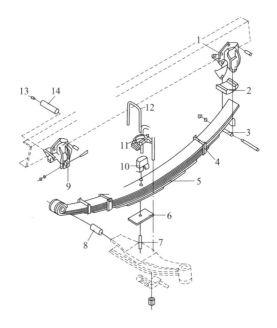

【参考视频】

图 13.7　Rigid axle suspension　非独立悬架

1—bracket 支架；2—sliding plate 滑板；3—set pin sleeve 限位销套；4—hoop holt 加紧螺栓；5—spring clamp 钢板弹簧；6—base plate 踏板；7—center blot 中心螺栓；8—spring bushings 弹簧销衬套；9—front bracket 前支架；10—limiting stopper 限位块；11—cover sheet 盖板；12—U-bolt U 形螺栓；13—grease fitting 润滑脂嘴；14—spring pin 钢板弹簧销

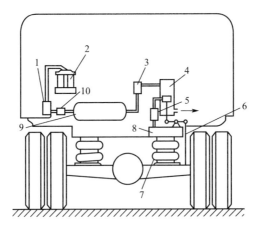

图 13.8　Air spring rigid-axle type suspension　空气弹簧非独立悬架

1—oil water separator 油水分离器；2—air compassion 空气压缩机；3、5—air filter 空气滤清器；4—vehicle height control 车身高度控制阀；6—control rod 控制杆；7—air spring 空气弹簧；8—air receiver 储气罐；9—air tank 储气筒；10—compression regulator 压力调节器

108

# Unit 13  AUTOMOBILE RUNNING GEAR

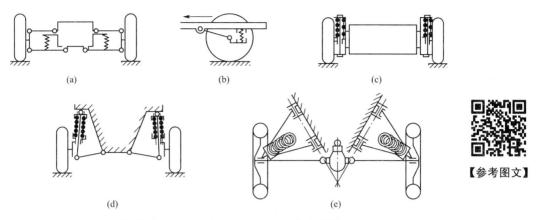

图 13.9  Independent suspension  独立悬架

(a) transverse link type independent suspension 横臂式独立悬架；(b) trailing arm type independent suspension 纵臂式独立悬架；(c) MacPherson strut suspension 麦弗逊滑柱式悬架；(d) MacPherson suspension 麦弗逊式悬架；
(e) single oblique arm type 单斜臂式独立悬架

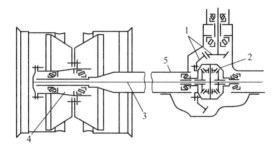

图 13.10  Undivided drive axle  非断开式驱动桥

1—final drive 主减速器；2—differential 差速器；3—axle shaft 半轴；
4—wheel hub 轮毂；5—driving axle housing 驱动桥壳

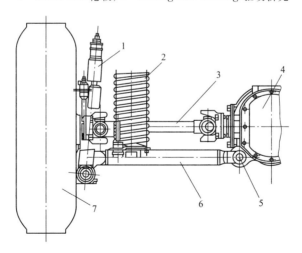

图 13.11  Divided drive axle  断开式驱动桥

1—shock absorber 减振器；2—spring element 弹性元件；3—axle shaft 半轴；
4—final drive 主减速器；5—swing arm shaft 摆臂轴；
6—swing arm 摆臂；7—wheel 车轮

## Reading Materials

### Passage 1

#### Running Gear

The functions of the automobile running gear are:

(1) Accepting the engine torque transmitted through the transmission system, and through the adhesion action between the driving wheel and the road surface producing the driving force of the road face to driving wheels and ensuring the car's normal running.

(2) Passing and enduring the road surface acting on the wheels' each direction reaction force and the torque they forming.

(3) As far as possible alleviating the shock to the body of the uneven road, and attenuating its vibration to ensure the vehicle ride comfor.

(4) Cooperating with the vehicle steering system. Coordinately, achieve the proper control of the direction of vehicle travel to ensure the vehicle handling stability.

#### Running Gear Components

Wheel type automobile running gear consists of frame, axle, wheel and suspension.

#### Frame

The functions of the frame are as follows:

(1) To carry the weight of the vehicle and its passengers.

(2) To withstand the engine and transmission torque and thrust stress, as well as accelerating and braking torques.

(3) To withstand the centrifugal force while cornering.

(4) To withstand the bending and twisting stress due to the rise and fall of the front and rear axles.

The frame is a load carrying beam structure consisting of two side members and several cross members. The frame is a base to which all main parts and units are fastened. The frame also includes brackets for mounting the fenders, footboard, fuel tank, springs, front bumper, two hooks and a pintle hook at the rear.

The frame of an automobile provides the support for the engine, body and transmission members. The frame transmits the load through suspension system and axles to the wheel.

#### Axle

Drive axle is located at the end of the power train. It mainly consists of the final drive, differential, axle shaft and drive axle housing.

The drive axle can be grouped into divided drive axle and undivided drive axle.

## Unit 13 AUTOMOBILE RUNNING GEAR

### Wheel and tires

To maintain grip when a vehicle is travelling at speed over a bumpy surface, a wheel must be light in weight. Also it must be strong, cheap to produce, easy to clean and simple to remove.

The wheel of an auto is composed of the wheel hub, the arm of wheel, the wheel rim and the pneumatic tire. It supports the weight of a car and distributes it over the road surface. It also transfers the force in every direction between the road and the auto body, which makes the car move.

Tires are important to your safety and comfort. They transmit the driving and braking power to the road. The car's direction control, road-ability and riding comfort are dependent on the tires. Tires should be selected and maintained with great care.

There are two basic types of tires-those with inner tubes and those without (called "tubeless" tires). Most modern automobile tires are of the tubeless type. Truck and bus tires are usually of the tube type.

### Suspension

The suspension system supports the weight of the engine, transmission, car body, and whatever the car body is carrying. This system has parts that link the wheels and tires to the frame or body.

The spring is the flexible component of the suspension and the key part of the suspension. They absorb the shocks of the road surface so that passenger have a comfortable ride. Basic types are: coil spring, leaf spring, torsion bar spring and air sprig.

The suspension system has two subsystems—the front suspension and the rear suspension. Modern cars use an independent front suspension. In this system, each wheel mounts separately to the frame and has its own individual spring and shock absorber. Thus, the wheels act independently of one another. When one wheel hits a bump or hole in the road, the other wheel does not deflect.

 阅读材料

**材料 1（参考译文）**

【参考视频】

### 行 驶 系 统

汽车行驶系统的功能有：

（1）接收由发动机经传动系统传来的转矩，并通过驱动轮与路面间的附着力作用，产生路面对驱动轮的驱动力，以保证汽车的正常行驶。

（2）传递并承受路面作用于车轮上的各向反力及其所形成的力矩。

（3）尽可能缓和不平路面对车身造成的冲击，并衰减其振动，以保证汽车行驶平顺。

(4) 与汽车转向系统协调地配合工作,实现汽车行驶方向的正确控制,以保证汽车操纵稳定性。

**行驶系统组成**

轮式汽车行驶系统一般由车架、车桥、车轮和悬架组成。

**车架**

车架的功能如下:
(1) 支撑车辆和乘客的重量。
(2) 承受发动机和变速器转矩和推力的压力,以及加速和制动力矩。
(3) 承受转弯时的离心力。
(4) 承受由于前桥和后桥上下振动产生弯曲和扭转应力。

车架是一个承载梁结构,由两个边梁和几个横梁组成。车架是固定所有主要部件和设备的一个基架。车架还包括安装挡泥板、踏板、油箱、弹簧、前保险杠、两个挂钩以及一个在后边的牵引钩的支架。

汽车的车架为发动机、车身和变速器部件提供了支持。车架把负荷通过悬架和车桥传递给车轮。

**车桥**

驱动桥位于传动系统的末端,它主要包括主减速器、差速器、半轴和驱动桥壳。

驱动桥分为整体式和断开式两种。

**车轮和轮胎**

当车辆在一个崎岖不平的路面上高速行驶时,为了保持附着力,车轮必须很轻。车轮还必须要结实,生产成本低廉,易于清洁,拆卸简单。

一个汽车的车轮由轮毂、轮辐、轮辋和充气轮胎组成。它支撑着一个汽车的重量并分布于道路表面。它还传输道路和车身之间各个方向的力,使汽车向前运动。

轮胎对乘客的安全性和舒适性来说非常重要,它们把驱动力和制动力传递到路面。汽车的方向控制、驾驶性能和乘坐舒适性都取决于轮胎,所以选择和维护轮胎时应非常小心。

轮胎有两种基本类型:有内胎的轮胎和没有内胎的轮胎(即所谓的"无内胎"轮胎)。大多数现代汽车的轮胎是无内胎的类型;货车和公共汽车的轮胎通常是有内胎的类型。

**悬架**

悬架系统支撑着发动机、变速器和车身的重量,以及车身承载的任何东西。该系统具有把车轮与轮胎和车架或车身连接起来的部件。

弹簧是悬架的弹性元件,并且是悬架的重要组成部分。它们吸收路面的冲击,使乘客乘坐舒适。其基本的类型有:螺旋弹簧、钢板弹簧、扭杆弹簧和空气弹簧。

悬架系统有两个子系统——前悬架和后悬架。现代汽车使用独立前悬架。在这个系统中,每个车轮单独地安装在车架上,有其各自的弹簧和减振器,因此,车轮彼此独立行事。当一个车轮在路面上碰到突起或小孔的时候,其他车轮不会受影响。

## Unit 13　AUTOMOBILE RUNNING GEAR

**Passage 2**

### Industry Overview

Frame and body are the key factors that affect the vehicle's ride comfort, handling stability and security like the suspension.

Although the frame-in-one takes the most of the current market, still some vehicles take the frame as a separate component. Body or cab mounted on the chassis through the elastic support reduces noise and vibration within the body.

There are a variety of frames currently such as girder type, integral type, tubular type and so on. Girder type is the earliest frame type. The advantage is to provide a strong load-bearing capacity and torsional stiffness, simple structure, easy development and less production process requirements. The disadvantage is the quality of the heavy steel beams—frames accounted for a substantial part of the entire vehicle weight. In addition, the thick beams run through the entire vehicle longitudinally, affecting vehicle layout and space utilization. The thickness of beam raises the platform of the passenger compartment and the cargo body installed on it, so the center of vehicle gravity is higher. Taking all these factors into account, we can see that beam-type frame is applicable to large-load truck, medium and large passenger cars, as well as frame stiffness demanding vehicles, such as off-road vehicles.

Automobile manufacturers have also developed aluminum alloy frame. The biggest advantage is its light aluminum alloy frame(the same stiffness of the case). But the costs are high, which is not suitable for mass production, not to mention the characteristics of aluminum alloy itself which shows its carrying capacity is restricted. Only a few of depots are used in small-scale, mass-produced sports cars, such as Lotus Elise and the Renault Spider.

Passive suspension, with simple structure, reliable performance, low cost, no energy consumption, is widely used. Although active suspension performance is better, the auto parts are expensive and energy consumption is high resulting limited work and application. Semi-active suspension performance is better than passive suspension, and the cost is much lower than active suspension. It is the main development direction of suspension system in the future.

## 材料2（参考译文）

### 行　业　概　况

车架与车身和悬架一样，是影响汽车的平顺性、操纵稳定性和安全性的重要因素。

虽然整体式车架占据了当前大部分市场，仍有一些车辆把车架看作单独的部件。车身或驾驶室通过弹性支架安装在底盘上以减少车身内部的噪声和振动。

现有的车架种类有大梁式、承载式、钢管式及特殊材料一体成形式等。大梁式是最早的车架类型，其优点是钢梁提供很强的承载能力和抗扭刚度，而且结构简单，开发容易，生产工艺的要求也较低。其缺点是钢制大梁质量沉重，车架质量占去全车总质量的相当大一部分；此外，粗壮的大梁纵贯全车，影响整车的布局和空间利用率，大梁的厚度使安装在其上的坐厢和货厢的地台升高，使整车重心偏高。综合这些因素可见，大梁式车架适用于要求有大载质量的货车、大中型客车，以及对车架刚度要求很高的车辆，如越野车。

汽车制造商也开发了铝合金车架。铝合金车架最大优点是轻（相同刚度的情况下）。但是它成本高，不宜大量生产，而且铝合金本身的特性决定了其承载能力受限制。暂时只有少数车厂将其运用在小型的量产跑车上，如莲花 Elise 和雷诺 Spider。

被动悬架由于结构简单，性能可靠，成本低，无能源消耗，所以被广泛使用。虽然主动悬架性能优越，但部件昂贵，能源消耗很高，所以在工作和应用时受到限制；半主动悬架性能优于被动悬架，成本远低于主动悬架，因此它是悬架系统未来主要的发展方向。

# Unit 14

# AUTOMOBILE STEERING SYSTEM
# 汽车转向系统

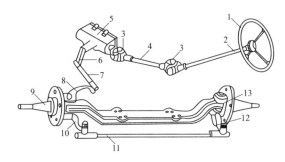

图 14.1　Manual steering system　机械转向系统

1—steering wheel 转向盘；2—steering shaft 转向轴；3—universal joint 转向万向节；4—steering inner articulated shaft 转向传动轴；5—steering gear 转向器；6—pitman arm 转向摇臂；7—steering drag rod 转向直拉杆；8—steering arm 转向节臂；9、13—steering knuckle 左右转向节；10、12—tie rod linkage 左右梯形臂；11—tie rod 转向横拉杆

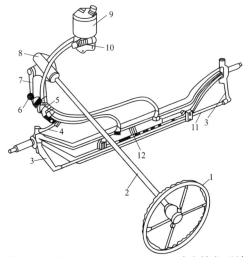

图 14.2　Power steering system　动力转向系统

1—steering wheel 转向盘；2—steering shaft 转向轴；3—tie rod linkage 梯形臂；4—steering primary rod 转向主拉杆；5—steering control valve 转向控制阀；6—steering knuckle 转向节；7—pitman arm 转向摇臂；8—manual steering gear 机械转向器；9—steering fuel tank 转向油罐；10—steering pump 转向油泵；11—tie rod 转向横拉杆；12—steering power cylinder 转向动力缸

【参考图文】

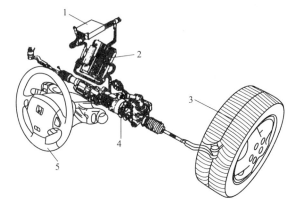

图 14.3 Electronic power steering system 电动式动力转向系统

1—control device 控制装置；2—power device 动力装置；3—steering wheel 转向轮；
4—motor 电动机；5—steering wheel 转向盘

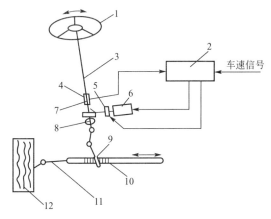

图 14.4 Alto electronic power steering 奥拓电动助力转向系统(EPS)

1—steering wheel 转向盘；2—electronic controller 电子控制器；3—steering shaft 转向轴；
4—torque sensor 转矩传感器；5—clutch 离合器；6—boosting motor 助力电动机；
7—torsion bar 扭力杆；8—output shaft 输出轴；9—steering gear 转向齿轮；
10—steering rack 转向齿条；11—tie rod 横拉杆；12—tyre 轮胎

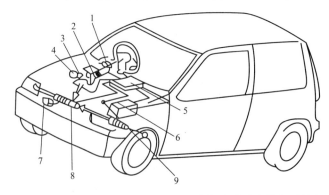

图 14.5 Alto electronic power steering 奥拓电动助力转向系统(EPS)

1—speed sensor 车速传感器；2—torque sensor 转矩传感器；3—retarder linkage 减速机构；4—motor clutch 电动机离合器；5—electronic controller 电子控制器；6—battery 蓄电池；7—generator 发电机；8—steering linkage 转向机构；9—engine speed sensor 发动机转速传感器

## Unit 14　AUTOMOBILE STEERING SYSTEM

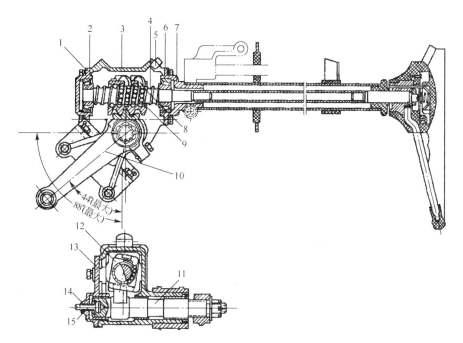

图 14.6　Recirculating ball steering system　循环球式转向器(北京 BJ212 型)

1—bottom cover 下盖；2、6—regulating gasket 调整垫片；3—housing 壳体；4—steering worm 转向蜗杆；5—steering plug 转向螺塞；7—head cover 上盖；8—ball pipeline 钢球导管；9—ball 钢球；10—pitman arm 转向摇臂；11—pitman arm shaft 转向摇臂轴；12—steering nut 转向螺母；13—side cover 侧盖；14—nut 螺母；15—adjuster bolt 调整螺栓

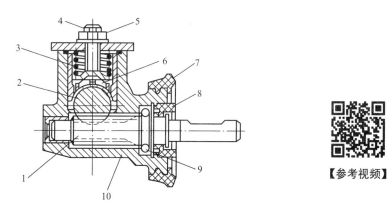

图 14.7　Rack and pinion steering system
齿轮齿条式转向器(红旗 CA7220 型轿车)

1—steering pinion 转向齿轮；2—steering rack 转向齿条；3—spring 弹簧；4—adjuster bolt 调整螺栓；5—nut 螺母；6—lock block 压块；7—shield cover 防尘罩；8—oil seal 油封；9—bearing 轴承；10—housing 壳体

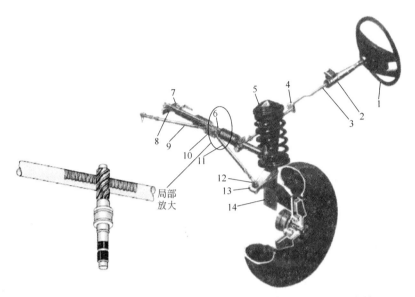

图 14.8　Red Flag CA7220‑car steering gear　红旗 CA7220 型轿车转向器

1—steering wheel 转向盘；2—steering column 转向柱管；3—steering shaft 转向轴；4—flexible coupling 柔性万向节；5—suspension assembly 悬架总成；6—steering gear 转向器；7—bracket 支架；8—steering shock absorber 转向减振器；9—right tie rod 右横拉杆；10—bracket 托架；11—left tie rod 左横拉杆；12—ball hinge 球铰链；13—steering knuckle arm 转向节臂；14—steering knuckle 转向节

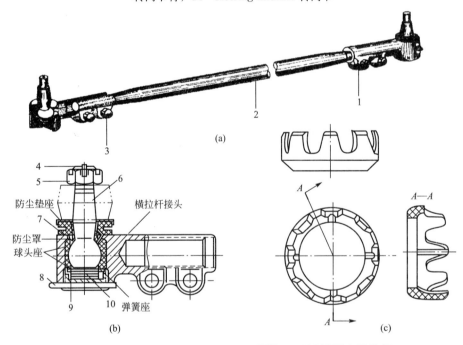

图 14.9　Jiefang‑CA1092 tie rod　解放 CA1092 型转向横拉杆

（a）tie rod 转向横拉杆；（b）joint 接头；（c）ball head seat 球头座

1—tie rod joint 横拉杆接头；2—tie rod housing 横拉杆体；3—fastening bolt 加紧螺栓；4—opening pin 开口销；5—nut 螺母；6—ball head pin 球头销；7—dust cover 防尘垫；8—limit pin 限位销；9—plug 螺塞；10—spring 弹簧

## Unit 14　AUTOMOBILE STEERING SYSTEM

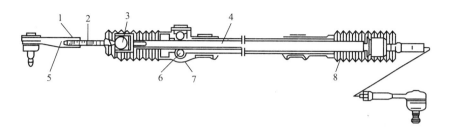

图 14.10　Steering linkage　天津夏利 TJ7100 型轿车的转向传动机构
1—fastening nut 锁紧螺母；2—tie rod 转向横拉杆；3—ball head 球头；
4—steering rack 转向齿条；5—tie rod joint 横拉杆接头；6—steering
pinion 转向齿轮；7—housing 壳体；8—dust cover 防尘罩

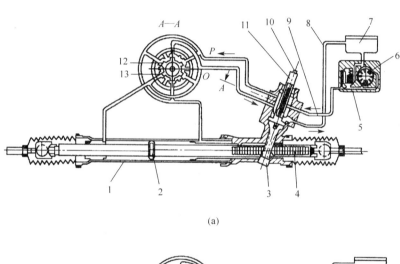

(a)

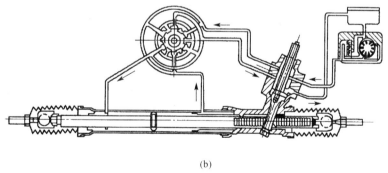

(b)

图 14.11　JETTA car integral boosting system　捷达轿车整体式助力转向器
(a) running in line 直线行驶时；(b) turning in motion 转弯行驶时
1—steering booster cylinder 转向助力缸；2—booster cylinder piston 助力缸活塞；3—steering
pinion 转向齿轮；4—steering rack 转向齿条；5—flow control valve(safety valve)流量控制阀
（带安全阀）；6—steering oil pump(impeller)转向油泵(叶片泵)；7—steering oil-reserve tank
转向储油罐；8—oil return pipeline 回油管路；9—oil inlet pipeline 进油管路；10—torsion
bar 扭杆；11—steering shaft 转向轴；12—valve spool 阀芯；13—valve sleeve 阀套

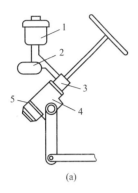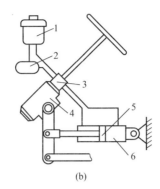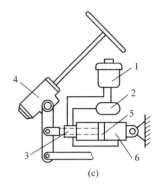

图 14.12 Boosting steering system types 助力转向系的几种类型

(a) integral boosting steering system 整体式助力转向系；(b) semi-integral boosting steering system 半整体式助力转向系；(c) modular boosting steering system 组合式助力转向系

1—steering oil tank 转向油罐；2—steering oil pump 转向油泵；3—steering control valve 转向控制阀；4—steering 转向器；5—booster cylinder piston 助力缸活塞；6—steering booster cylinder 转向助力缸

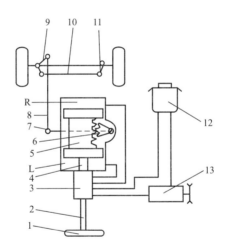

图 14.13 Hydraulic boosting steering system 液压助力转向系统

1—steering wheel 转向盘；2—steering shaft 转向轴；3—steering control valve 转向控制阀；4—steering worm 转向螺杆；5—rack 齿条；6—sector rack 扇齿；7—pitman arm 摇臂；8—steering tie rod 转向主拉杆；9—steering knuckle 转向节；10—steering tie rod 转向横拉杆；11—tie rod type arm 转向梯形臂；12—steering oil tank 转向油罐；13—steering oil pump 转向油泵

## Reading Materials

### Steering System

The purpose of the steering system is guiding the car where the driver wants it to go. It consists of steering wheel, steering shaft, worm, sector gear, pitman arm, drag rod,

# Unit 14　AUTOMOBILE STEERING SYSTEM

steering knuckle, king pin, tie rod, front axle and steering knuckle. They enable the car to change the direction by means of turning and moving forth and back.

The basic steering system in most cars is the same. The steering gear is the heart of the steering system. This usually is next to the engine. A shaft extends from the back of the steering gear. This shaft is connected to the steering column or steering shaft. It goes through the firewall and into the passenger compartment. The steering wheel is at the top of the steering column. Another shaft comes from the bottom of the steering gear. This shaft connects to the arms, rods, and links. This parts assembly, called the steering linkage, connects the steering gear to the parts at the wheel. The wheel and tires mount to the steering knuckles. The knuckles are pivoted at the top and bottom. Thus, the wheel and tires can turn from side to side.

While the steering system may look complicated, it works quite simply. When a driver drives a car straight down the road, the steering gear is centered. The gear holds the linkage centered so that the wheels and tires point straight ahead. When the driver turns the steering wheel, the steering shaft rotates and the steering gear moves toward that side. The shaft coming out the bottom of the steering gear turns, as well, when the shaft turns, it pulls the linkage to one side and makes the steering knuckles turn slightly about their pivot point. Thus, the steering knuckle, kingpin, wheels, and tires turn to one side, causing the car to turn.

The line, or axis, about which the steering knuckles rotate is called the steering axis. When a car has completed the turn, the steering wheel returns to the center position. As a result, the steering gear pulls the linkage, wheels, and tires back to the center. The car now resumes its straight-ahead travel.

There are several different types of steering gears. There are, however, only two types of steering systems: manual steering systems and power steering systems.

In the manual type, the driver does all the work of turning the steering wheel, steering gear, wheels, tires. In the power type, hydraulic fluid assists the operation so that driver effort is reduced. Power steering systems were introduced in the early 1950s. Most new cars have power steering.

Two types of steering gears are used, the recirculating ball and the rack-and-pinion.

Most large cars use the recirculating ball type of steering gear. This steering gear is durable, with good steering response and good road feel for the driver. The gear has a grooved shaft called the worm-shaft. A large block, called the ball nut or worm nut, has teeth on one side and fits over the worm-shaft. A number of small steel balls fit between the worm-shaft and the ball nut. Small tubes on the ball nut serve as ball guides. These ball rides in the grooves on the worm-shaft. Bearings and seals fit on each end of the worm-shaft. An adjusting plug at one end allows a mechanic to adjust the worm-shaft. A steering gear housing covers the parts.

In the steering gear, the output shaft makes less revolution than the input shaft. In the recirculating ball steering gear, the worm-shaft is the input shaft. The worm-shaft connects to the steering column. The pitman shaft is like the output shaft of the steering gear, which connects to the pitman arm on the steering linkage.

The recirculating ball system is the mechanical part of this steering gear. A number of steel balls fit into grooves on the worm-shaft and into similar grooves inside the ball nut. Therefore, the ball nut does not actually ride on the worm-shaft. Rather, it rides on the steel balls between the two parts.

As the worm-shaft turns, the balls move the ball nut up and down along the worm-shaft. This turns the sector shaft, since the sector teeth mesh with the ball nut teeth.

The movement of the balls moves the ball nut and turns the sector shaft. The ball guides recirculate the balls through the grooves between the worm-shaft and ball nut.

Rack-and-pinion steering is used on many new smaller cars and on most cars with a transverse engine. This steering gear is small and lightweight. It provides good steering with minimum driver effort. In addition, rack-and-pinion steering needs fewer parts in the steering gear linkage. Thus, it is easy to service, rack-and-pinion steering gives more feedback and road feel to the driver. If the steering is not power assisted, more driver effort is needed for rack-and-pinion steering when it is used in heavy cars.

The rack-and-pinion system has two main parts—the pinion and the rack. The pinion is on the end of the steering wheel turns the pinion. The rack is a flat bar with teeth on one side. The rack teeth mesh with the teeth on the pinion. The rack is crosswise between the front wheels. This system has no output shaft. Instead, rotation of the pinion moves the rack from left to right and right to left. The motion of the rack causes the steering linkage to move back and forth because the rack is part of the linkage. The steering linkage then causes the wheels to turn to the left or right.

Like recirculating ball steering gears, rack-and-pinion gears have steering ration. Again, the ratio shows the relationship between the motion of the steering wheel and the motion of the four wheels.

To make car easier to drive, hydraulic fluid is used to assist the steering system. The integral power steering system is one of the popular power steering system in use. Over the years, power steering has become a standard equipment item on many large domestic models. With that, and the optional demand for this system, power steering is installed on over 90 percent of all domestic new cars in the United States and some other developed western countries. Most late model passenger cars with power steering use either a power rack and pinion system, or an integral power steering gear assembly. All systems require a power steering pump attached to the engine and driven by a belt, a pressure hose assembly, and a return line. In addition, a control valve is incorporated somewhere in the hydraulic circuit.

# Unit 14  AUTOMOBILE STEERING SYSTEM

## 阅读材料（参考译文）

### 转 向 系 统

【参考视频】

转向系统的作用是根据驾驶员的意图改变行驶方向。转向系统包括转向盘、转向轴、蜗杆、齿扇、转向摇臂、直拉杆、转向节、主销、转向横拉杆、前轴和转向节，通过前后转动和运动可以改变汽车行驶方向。

基本的转向系统在大多数汽车上是相同的。转向器是转向系统的核心，通常它位于发动机旁边。一根轴接在转向器的后面和转向柱或转向轴连接，转向轴通过驾驶室隔板到达驾驶室内，转向盘在转向柱的顶端。另外一根轴连接在转向器的底部，连接转向摇臂和连杆，这部分总成称为转向传动装置，也是连接转向器和车轮的装置。车轮和轮胎安装在转向节上，车轮和轮胎绕着转向节的顶部和底部从一侧转动到另一侧。

转向系统看起来很复杂，但工作很简单。当驾驶者驱车沿着道路直线行驶时，转向器处在中间位置，转向器使连杆处在中间位置使得车轮处于直线状态；当驾驶者转动转向盘时，转向轴转动使得转向器朝一边运动，转向摇臂也跟着运动，使得转向节绕着旋转中心转动，这样转向节、主销、车轮和轮胎转向一边，汽车实现转向。

转向节绕其旋转的轴称为主销，以后再讨论主销。当汽车完成转向以后，转向盘回到中间位置，转向器拉着连杆装置、车轮和轮胎回到中间位置，汽车将重新开始直线行驶。

转向器可以分为两种不同类型：机械式转向器和动力式转向器。

在机械式转向器中，全部依靠驾驶者转动转向盘、转向器、车轮和轮胎；而在动力式转向器中，液压协助驾驶员操作，减轻驾驶员的操作强度。动力式转向器在20世纪50年代被使用，现在大多数轿车都采用动力式转向器。

经常采用两种类型的转向器：循环球式和齿轮齿条式转向器。

大多数大型汽车采用循环球式转向器。这种转向器耐用，转向灵敏并且让驾驶员有好的路感。这种转向器有一个开槽的轴，称为蜗杆轴，转向螺母的一侧有齿形，和蜗杆轴相啮合，在蜗杆轴和转向螺母之间安装有大量的钢球。在转向螺母中导管起着引导作用，这些钢球在蜗杆槽内运动。轴承和油封安装在蜗杆轴的两端，在蜗杆轴一端有调整垫片可以机械地调节蜗杆轴，所有这些部分都装在转向器壳体内。

在转向器中，输出轴的转速比输入轴慢。在循环球转向器中，蜗杆轴为输入轴，蜗杆轴和转向柱连接，摇臂轴是转向器的输出轴。摇臂轴和转向传动机构的转向摇臂相连。

循环球系统是转向器的机械部分，很多钢球安装在蜗杆轴和转向螺母的槽内，然而转向螺母和蜗杆轴并不直接接触运动，而是依靠钢球在其之间进行运动。

当蜗杆轴转动时，钢球使得转向螺母在蜗杆上上下运动，进而转动齿扇轴，因为齿扇轴上的齿和转向螺母上的齿是相互啮合的。

钢球的运动移动转向螺母并且转动齿扇轴，钢球通过蜗杆轴和转向螺母之间的沟槽引导转向螺杆运动。

齿轮齿条式转向器常用在小型汽车和横置发动机的汽车上。这种转向器体积小，质量小，转向轻便。另外，其连接装置需要更少的部件，因此维修方便，并且能给驾驶员以好的反馈和路感。在重型车上如果不采用动力转向器，则驾驶员操作起来会很吃力。

齿轮齿条转向器有两个主要部件——齿轮和齿条。齿轮安装在转向盘的末端，转向盘使得齿轮转动，齿条是一个平的杆，在其一面有齿，齿条的齿和齿轮上的齿相啮合。齿条横向安装，这种系统没有输出轴，齿轮的旋转使得齿条左右运动。因为齿条是连接装置的一部分，所以齿条的左右运动引起转向连接装置前后运动，转向连接装置引起车轮左右运动。

像循环球式转向器一样，齿轮齿条式转向器也有转向传动比，其传动比指的是转向盘的运动速度和汽车四个车轮的转速之间的比例。

为了使汽车更容易操纵，常用液压助力协助转向系统。常用的动力转向系是整体式动力转向系统。多年来，在国内许多大型乘用车上动力转向系已经变成了一个标准的配置。基于这样的情况和这种系统的可选择性，在美国和一些西方发达国家，90%的新型乘用车都安装了动力转向器。大多数最新的乘用车动力转向器都采用动力齿轮齿条式系统或整体式动力转向器总成。所有这些系统必须有一个和发动机相连接并且通过一个传动带驱动的液压泵、一个压力管路总成和回油管，另外，在液压回路中还需要一个控制阀。

【参考视频】

# Unit 15

# AUTOMOBILE BRAKE SYSTEM
# 汽车制动系统

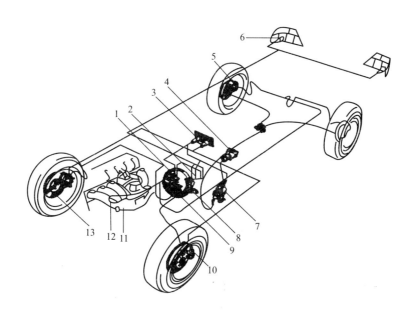

图 15.1　Automobile brake system　汽车制动系统

1—brake booster 制动助力器；2—brake light switch 制动灯开关；3—parking brake and moving beacon 驻车制动与行车制动警告灯；4—parking brake uninstalling equipment 驻车制动解除装置；5—rear brake 后轮制动器；6—brake light 制动灯；7—parking brake pedal 驻车制动踏板；8—brake pedal 制动踏板；9—brake master cylinder 制动主缸；10—brake pliers 制动钳；11—engine inlet pipe 发动机进气管；12—low pressure pipe 低压管；13—brake disc 制动盘

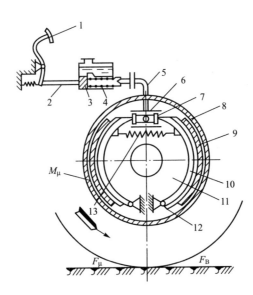

图 15.2　Operating principle of brake system
制动系传动原理

1—brake pedal 制动踏板；2—push rod 推杆；3—master cylinder piston 主缸活塞；4—brake master cylinder 制动主缸；5—oil pipe 油管；6—brake wheel cylinder 制动轮缸；7—wheel cylinder piston 轮缸活塞；8—brake drum 制动鼓；9—friction lining 摩擦片；10—brake shoe 制动蹄；11—brake plate 制动底板；12—anchor pin 支承销；13—brake shoe return spring 制动蹄回位弹簧

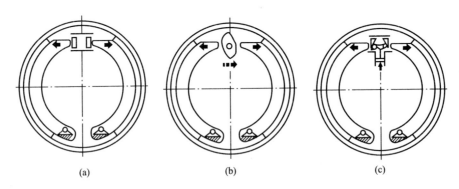

图 15.3　Types of brake actuating equipment 各类型制动器促动装置
（a）wheel cylinder 轮缸式；（b）cam 凸轮式；（c）wedge 楔块式

# Unit 15 AUTOMOBILE BRAKE SYSTEM

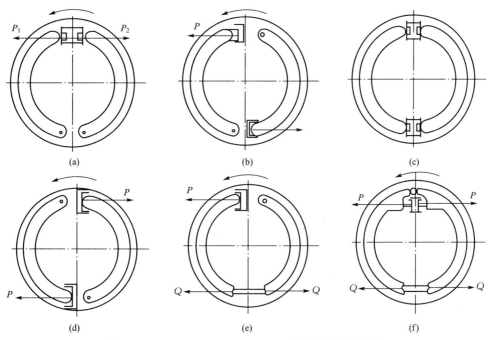

图 15.4 Drum brake classification 鼓式制动器的分类

(a) leading trailing shoe brake 领从蹄式；(b) two leading shoe brake 双领蹄式；
(c) duo two leading shoe brake 双向双领蹄式；(d) two trailing shoe brake 双从蹄式；
(e) uni-servo brake 单向自增力式；(f) duo-servo brake 双向自增力式

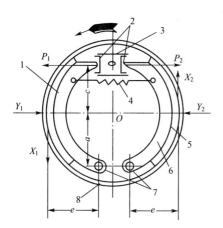

图 15.5 Simple imbalance brake(leading-trailing)
简单非平衡式制动器(领从蹄式)

1—left brake shoe 左制动蹄；2—wheel cylinder piston 轮缸活塞；3—brake wheel cylinder 制动轮缸；4—return spring 回位弹簧；5—friction lining 摩擦片；6—right brake shoe 右制动蹄；7—anchor pin 支承销；8—brake drum 制动鼓

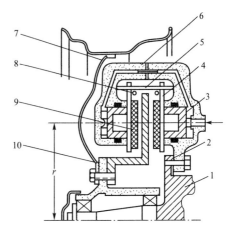

图 15.6 Caliper disc brake(fixed caliper)
钳盘式制动器结构图(定钳盘式)

1—knuckle 转向节或桥壳；2—adjusting shim 调整垫片；3—piston ring 活塞；4—brake block 制动块；5—guidance anchor pin 导向支承销；6—caliper housing 钳体；7—disc 轮盘；8—return ring 回位弹簧；9—brake disc 制动盘；10—hub flange 轮毂凸缘；$r$—brake disc friction radius 制动盘摩擦半径

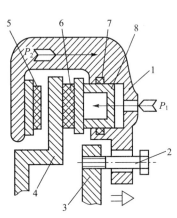

图 15.7　Principle of moving caliper brake structure
浮钳盘式制动器的结构

1—brake caliper housing 制动钳体；2—guide pin 导向销；3—brake anchor bracket 制动支架；
4—brake disc 制动盘；5—fixed brake block 固定制动块；6—actuating brake block 活动制动块；7—piston ring seal 活塞密封圈；8—piston 活塞

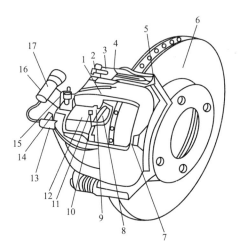

图 15.8　Disc brake with floating caliper structure
浮钳盘式制动器结构

1—brake caliper housing 制动钳体；2—fastening screw 紧固螺钉；3—guide pin 导向销；4—protection sleeve 防护套；5—brake caliper bracket 制动钳支架；6—brake disc 制动盘；7—fixed brake block 固定制动块；8—abatement shim 消声片；9—boot 防尘套；10—actuating brake block 活动制动块；11—seal 密封圈；12—piston ring 活塞；13—wire guide 电线导向夹；14—bleeder screw 放气螺钉；15—bleeder screw cap 放气螺钉帽；16—alarm switch 报警开关；17—clamp 电线夹

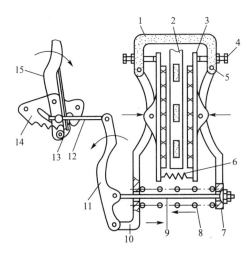

图 15.9　Shoe disc brake and its actuator structure　蹄盘式制动器及其传动机构

1—anchor bracket 支架；2—brake disc 制动盘；3—brake shoe 制动蹄；4—adjusting screw 调整螺钉；5—pin 销；6—tension spring 拉簧；7—back brake shoe arm 后制动蹄臂；
8—fixed spring 定位弹簧；9—shoe arm connecting rod 蹄臂拉杆；10—front-brake shoe arm 前制动蹄臂；11—connecting rod arm 拉杆臂；12—drive connecting rod 传动拉杆；13—ratchet 棘爪；14—sector 齿扇；15—parking brake rod 驻车制动杆

## Unit 15  AUTOMOBILE BRAKE SYSTEM

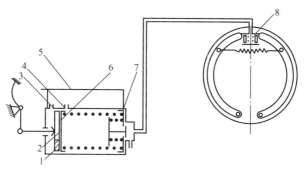

图 15.10  Hydraulic simple brake actuator  液压式简单制动传动机构
1—axial hole 轴向小孔；2—piston 活塞；3—compensator 补偿孔；4—bypass hole 旁通孔；5—brake pump 制动总泵；6—cup 皮碗；7—dual valve 双向阀；8—wheel braking cylinder 制动分泵(轮缸)

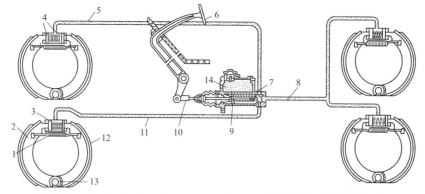

图 15.11  Single-line braking actuator device  单管路液压制动传动装置
1—return spring 回位弹簧；2、12—brake shoe 制动蹄；3—wheel cylinder 轮缸；4、9—piston 活塞；5、8、11—oil pipe 油管；6—brake pedal 制动踏板；7—brake master cylinder 主缸；10—plunger 推杆；13—anchor pin 支承销；14—braking fluid 制动液

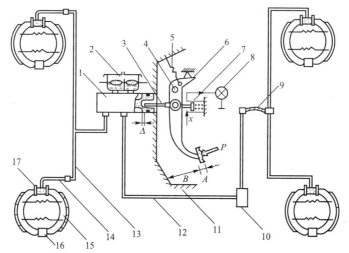

图 15.12  Dual hydraulic braking actuator  双管路液压制动传动装置
1—brake master cylinder 制动主缸；2—oil tank 储油罐；3—plunge 推杆；4—anchor pin 支承销；5—return spring 回位弹簧；6—brake pedal 制动踏板；7—brake light switch 制动灯开关；8—indicator light 指示灯；9—soft pipe 软管；10—proportioning valve 比例阀；11—floor 地板；12—rear axle pipe 后桥油管；13—front axle pipe 前桥油管；14—soft pipe 软管；15—brake shoe 制动蹄；16—anchor 支承座；17—wheel cylinder 轮缸；$\Delta$—free gap 自由间隙；$A$—free play 自由行程；$B$—effective stroke 有效行程

129

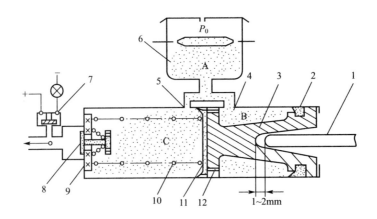

图 15.13 Hydraulic brake master cylinder(single cavity) 液压式制动主缸(单腔)

1—pushing rod 推杆；2—seal 密封圈；3—piston 活塞；4—inlet hole 进油孔；5—compensating hole 补偿孔；6—oil chamber 储油室；7—oil voltage brake switch 油压制动开关；8—oil outlet valve 出油阀；9—回油阀座；10—return spring 回位弹簧；11—cup 皮碗；12—axial hole 轴向孔；A—oil chamber 储油室；B—compensating oil chamber 补油室；C—pressure chamber 压力室

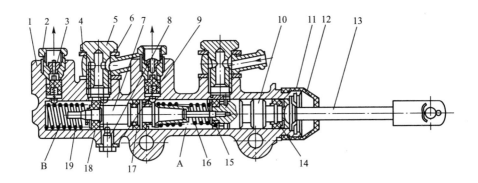

图 15.14 Dual master brake cylinder 双腔制动主缸

1—cylinder body 缸体；2—oil outlet pipe joint 出油管接头；3—nozzle oil outlet valve 嘴式出油阀；4—oil inlet pipe joint 进油管接头；5—hollow screw 空心螺钉；6—seal gasket 密封垫；7—front piston 前活塞；8—limit screw 限位螺钉；9—seal gasket 密封垫；10—back piston 后活塞；11—retaining plate 挡板；12—cap 护罩；13—push rod 推杆；14—back piston seal gasket 后活塞密封圈；15—back piston cup 后活塞皮碗；16—back piston return spring 后活塞回位弹簧；17—front piston seal gasket 前活塞密封圈；18—front piston cup 前活塞皮碗；19—front piston return spring 前活塞回位弹簧；B、A— front and back pressure chamber 前后压力室

## Unit 15  AUTOMOBILE BRAKE SYSTEM

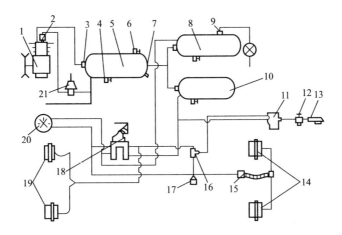

图 15.15  Dual circuit baric brake transmission structure  双回路气压制动传动机构

1—air compressors 空气压缩机；2—unloading valve 卸荷阀；3—one-way valve 单向阀；4—low-off valve 放水阀；5—air-reserve tank 储气筒；6—retaining air valve 取气阀；7—safty valve 安全阀；8—rear axle air-reserve tank 后桥储气筒；9—under baric alarm switch 气压过低报警开关；10—front axle air-reserve tank 前桥储气筒；11—trailer brake control valve 挂车制动控制阀；12—separating valve 分离阀；13—connecting point 连接头；14—rear wheel brake air chamber 后轮制动气室；15—quick release valve 快放阀；16—dual way check valve 双通单向阀；17—brake light switch 制动灯开关；18—brake control valve 制动控制阀；19—front wheel brake air chamber 前轮制动气室；20—barometer 气压表；21—pressure-regulator valve 调压阀

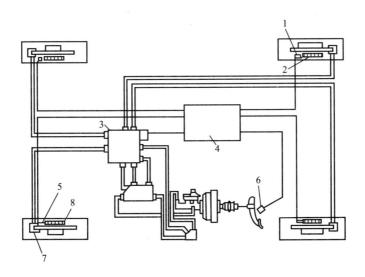

图 15.16  A typical ABS  典型 ABS(防抱死制动系统)

1—rear wheel speed sensor 后轮速度传感器；2、8—sensor rotor 传感器转子；3—ABS actuator ABS 执行器；4—ABS electronic control unit ABS 电子控制单元；5—front wheel speed sensor 前轮速度传感器；6—brake light switch 制动灯开关；7—disc brake pump 盘式车轮制动分泵

## Reading Materials

### Passage 1

#### Brake System

The automobile brake system is mainly used for helping the driver control the deceleration of the vehicle. It is one of the crucial systems, which is especially designed for decreasing the speed of the fast moving vehicle. A typical automotive brake system comprises of a brake device having different components, which are used for slowing or stopping down a vehicle. More precisely, these devices decrease or stop the speed of a moving or rotating body by absorbing kinetic energy mechanically or electrically. These automotive brake systems automatically control wheel slips and prevent the wheels from spinning. They are widely used in motor vehicles, buses, trucks, trains, airplanes, passenger coaches, trailers, and other types of automobiles.

Automobile brake system used in automobiles has come a long way in recent years. The adoption of antilock braking systems along with the introduction of different brake parts made of carbon fiber, steel, aluminum etc. have really provided better stopping performance in comparison with traditional ones. The major manufacturers of auto brake systems in the world are Bosch, Toyota and so on. Automotive brake parts fitted in the automobiles are critical to the controlled reduction of speed. These comprises of different types of supplementary parts, devices and accessories like brake booster, brake cylinders, brake lines etc. used in the automotive brake system for slowing down a moving vehicle by transferring the energy of momentum with the help of friction.

Automotive brake parts are long lasting, sturdy, corrosion resistant, and easy to assemble. Steel is the preferred metal for manufacturing these parts for automobiles. The other high performance materials that are used for producing brake parts and components are stainless steel, iron, copper, titanium, carbon steel, chromium, vanadium, cast iron, brass, bronze, aluminum, rubber and plastic.

 阅读材料

材料 1（参考译文）

制 动 系 统

汽车制动系统主要用来帮助驾驶员控制车辆减速。它是一个非常关键的系统，这个系统主要用来降低高速运动车辆的速度。典型的汽车制动系统使用包括不同组件的制动设备去降低汽车速度或使汽车停止，更精确地说是这些设备通过机械方式或电动方式吸收运动能量去降低汽车速度或使汽车停止，这些制动系统自动控制车轮滑行或阻止车轮旋转。制动系统广泛用于摩托车、公共汽车、货车、火车、飞机、

## Unit 15  AUTOMOBILE BRAKE SYSTEM

客车、拖车或其他类型汽车。

最近几年汽车制动系统取得了重大进展。防抱死制动系统(ABS)的采用提供了比传统制动系统更好的制动性能。防抱死制动系统的各部件采用碳纤维、钢和铝等制成。世界上汽车制动系统的主要制造商是博世公司、丰田公司等。汽车上安装的制动部件对控制汽车速度是非常关键的。这些部件包括不同种类的额外部件、设备或附件,像制动助力器、制动轮缸、制动管路等。这些部件用在汽车上利用摩擦消耗汽车机械能量,达到降低汽车速度的目的。

汽车制动部件应当是耐久的、坚固的和抗腐蚀的,并且要容易安装。通常使用钢来制造这些部件,其他用来制造这些制动部件的高性能材料有不锈钢、铁、铜、钛、碳钢、铬、钒、铸铁、黄铜、青铜、铝、橡胶和塑料。

Passage 2

### Brake Components

From drum brakes to power-assisted brakes, braking systems have been critical to automobiles and have continuously evolved with them. Today many path braking technologies and brake components such as brake boosters, brake cylinders, brake hydraulic valve, brake lines, etc. lend a braking system high efficacy. The anti-lock braking system has become very popular. The following are some braking systems and their components.

### Disc brakes

Disc brakes make use of friction to slow or stop an automobile. Disc brakes comprise brake pads that serve as friction material and are fixed onto a device called a brake caliper.

When the brake pedal is pushed by a driver the brake pads are mechanically, hydraulically, pneumatically or electromagnetically forced against both sides of the disc mounted on the wheels, thus regulating the speed.

### Drum Brakes

Drum brakes regulate speed by causing friction between the wheels and a set of shoes or pads that push against the inside surface of a rotating drum. The drum is attached to the rotating wheels. Typically, drum brakes are classified as either leading/trailing or twin leading. Out of the these types, the twin leading drum brakes are more effective.

### Parking Brakes

Parking brakes are normally used to keep an automobile stationary, when not being driven. Also known as emergency brake, hand brake, the brakes are often configured on the floor and between front passenger and the driver. However, they can even be configured as a lever at the bottom of the dashboard, or as a foot-operated pedal. The brake comprises a cable that connects the braking system at one end and a lever on the other. The driver operates the hand-lever(or a pedal) to actuate or release the brake.

### Brake Components

#### Brake Booster

A brake booster is a useful braking system component that enhances braking performance by augmenting the pressure applied when a brake pedal is pushed. When the engine is running it produces vacuum, a brake booster collects this vacuum through a rubber hose and uses it to amplify braking power. So even when the brake pedal is pushed only lightly, which causes more braking action, making the brakes more sensitive.

#### Brake Pedal

A brake pedal is a foot operated pedal. When it is pushed by the drivers, a piston moves in the master brake cylinder to regulate the speed of an automobile.

#### Brake Cylinder

An automobile's brake cylinder or a wheel cylinder is a component found in drum brake systems. It is at each of the wheels. Its function is to exert pressure onto the shoes so as to enable a contact between the shoes and the drum, thus actuating a braking action.

#### Other Brake Components

Other essential brake components include, brake hydraulic valve, brake lines, brake pumps and so on.

 材料2（参考译文）

## 制 动 组 件

【参考视频】　　从鼓式动力制动系统看，制动系统对汽车是非常关键的，并且不断演化出其他制动系统。如今许多制动技术和制动组件，例如，制动助力器、制动主缸、制动液压阀、制动管路等已经使得制动系统的效率变得很高，尤其是防抱死制动系统已经得到了广泛使用。下面介绍制动系统及其组件。

### 制动盘

制动盘利用摩擦力降低汽车速度或使汽车停止。盘式制动器包括一个制动摩擦衬块，该衬块充当摩擦材料并安装在制动钳上。

当驾驶员踩下制动踏板时，制动摩擦衬块被机械力、液压、气压或电磁力推向安装在车轮上的制动盘两侧的面上，从而控制速度。

### 制动鼓

鼓式制动器通过车轮和制动蹄或制动摩擦衬块之间产生的摩擦力去控制车速，制动蹄压向一个旋转的制动鼓内侧。制动鼓安装在旋转的车轮上。通常情况下，鼓式制动器分为领蹄式、从蹄式或双领蹄式，在这几种类型中双领蹄式效率更高。

## Unit 15　AUTOMOBILE BRAKE SYSTEM

### 驻车制动

驻车制动是在汽车没有被驱动时用来保持汽车静止的，又称紧急制动、手制动。驻车制动经常布置在乘客和驾驶员之间的地板上，它们经常在仪表板下部被设计成一个杠杆或者一个脚踩踏板。在驻车制动系统上一根拉索的一端连接在制动系统上，另一端连接在操作杆上，驾驶员通过操作操作杆(或一个踏板)去施加制动或解除制动。

### 制动组件

### 制动助力器

制动助力器是一个有用的制动系统部件，它通过提高制动踏板的推力提高制动性能。当发动机工作的时候产生真空度，制动助力器通过橡胶软管收集真空，并且用真空提高制动能力。因此只要驾驶员轻轻一推，就会产生更多的制动力，使制动系统更加灵敏。

### 制动踏板

制动踏板是一个脚踩的踏板。驾驶员踩下制动踏板，使制动主缸的活塞移动去控制汽车的速度。

### 制动主缸

汽车的制动主缸或制动轮缸用在鼓式制动器中。制动轮缸安装在每个车轮上，它的功能是施加压力到制动蹄上以使制动蹄和制动鼓接触产生制动。

【参考视频】

### 其他制动组件

其他必须的制动组件包括制动液压阀、制动管路、制动泵等。

# Unit 16

# AUTOMOBILE ELECTRICAL SYSTEM
# 汽车电气系统

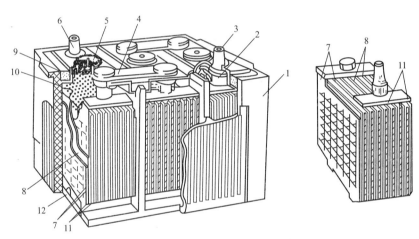

图 16.1　Battery　蓄电池的构造

1—battery housing 蓄电池外壳；2—electrode bush 电极衬套；3—positive post 正极柱；4—connecting bar 连接条；5—charger plug 加液孔螺塞；6—negative post 负极柱；7—negative plate 负极板；8—separator 隔板；9—sealant 封料；10—shield plate 护板；11—positive plate 正极板；12—rib 肋条

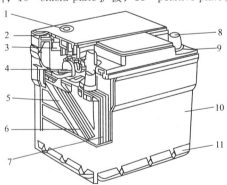

图 16.2　Repairless battery　免维护蓄电池的结构

1—interior microdensitometer 内装小型密度计；2—smoke hole 排烟孔；3—separator 隔板；4—central plate and cell connection bar 中心极板连接夹板和单格电池连接器；5—high density active substance 高密度活性物质；6—the small window forged on the lead-calcium grid 铅钙栅架上锻制的小窗；7—separator cover 密封极板的隔板封皮；8—post 极柱；9—lateral code number 横压代号；10—polypropylene shell 聚丙烯壳体；11—the downslide surface 用于安装的下滑面

# Unit 16  AUTOMOBILE ELECTRICAL SYSTEM

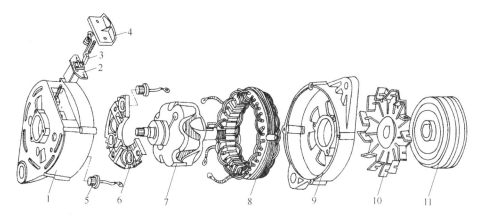

图 16.3  Domestic JF1813Z alternating generator  国产 JF1813Z 型交流发电机的结构

1—rear end cover 后端盖；2—brush holder 电刷架；3—brush 电刷；
4—brush spring housing 电刷弹簧压盖；5—silicondiode 硅二极管；
6—heating plate 散热板；7—rotor 转子；8—stator assembly 定子总成；
9—front housing 前端盖；10—fan 风扇；11—pulley 带轮

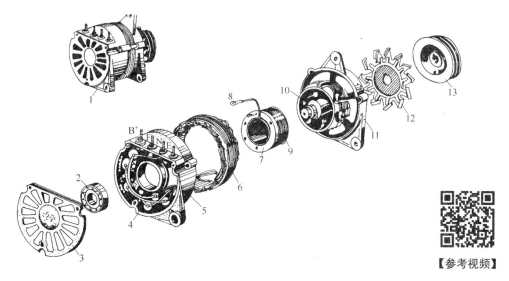

【参考视频】

图 16.4  JFW14X type brushless alternator (schematic)
国产 JFW14X 型爪极式无刷交流发电机外形及其分解图

1—outer shape 外形；2—back bearing 后轴承；3—shield cover 防护罩；4—conductive element
plate and diode 元件板及二极管；5—excitation winding bracket and back bearing bracket
磁场线圈支架及后轴承支架；6—stator assembly 定子总成；7—yoke of the magnet
磁轭；8—field coil joint 磁场线圈接头；9—field coil 磁场线圈；10—claw
pole and rotor assembly 爪极及转子轴总成；11—front housing 前端盖；
12—fan 风扇；13—driving pulley 传动带轮

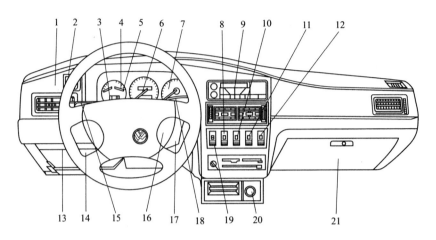

**图 16.5 SANTANA2000GSI type gauge board 桑塔纳 2000GSI 型轿车仪表板**

1—air outlet 出风口；2—light switch and board light regulator 灯光开关及仪表照明调节器；
3—electronic clock 电子钟；4—coolant temperature and gage 冷却液温度和油量表；
5—signal light 信号灯；6—odograph 车速里程表；7—tachometer 转速表；
8—alternate switch 备用开关灯；9—radio-cassette 收放机；10—fog light switch 雾灯开关；
11—back window heating switch 后窗加热器开关；12—hazard warning lamp switch 危险报警灯开关；
13—fuse shield plate shell 熔丝护板壳；14—choke button 阻风门按钮；15—steering signal light switch 转向信号灯；16—horn button 喇叭按钮；17—ignition switch 转向器锁/点火开关；
18—wiper and washer shifter lever switch 刮水器及洗涤器拨杆开关；
19—air condition switch 空调装置开关；20—cigarette lighter 点烟器；21—service box 杂物箱

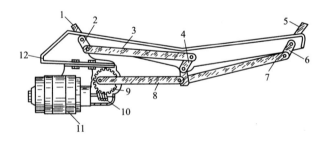

**图 16.6 Electrical wiper 电动刮水器**

1、5—electric wiper bracket 刮片架；2、4、6—bracket 摆架；3、7、8—tie bar 拉杆；9—wormgear 蜗轮；
10—worm 蜗杆；11—DC motor with permanent magnets 永磁式直流电动机；12—bracket 支架

# Unit 16  AUTOMOBILE ELECTRICAL SYSTEM

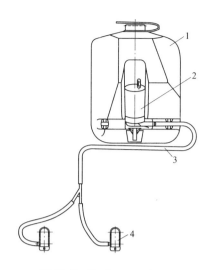

图 16.7  Santana washer
桑塔纳洗涤器

1—fluid-reserve tank 储液罐；
2—washing pump 洗涤泵；
3—water delivery pipe
输水软管；4—nozzle 喷嘴

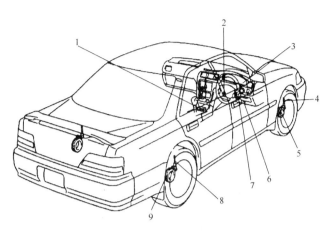

图 16.8  Tyre pressure alarm system  轮胎气压报警系统

1—engine control system computer 发动机控制系统计算机；
2—parking light switch 驻车灯开关；3—tyre pressure alarm
轮胎气压报警；4、8—wheel speed sensor 车轮速度传感器；
6—set switch 设定开关；7—tyre pressure alarm
system computer 轮胎气压报警系统计算机；
5、9—speed sensor steering wheel 速度传感器转盘

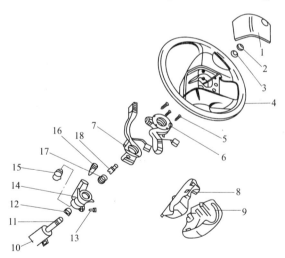

图 16.9  JETTA steering column combination switch  捷达转向柱组合开关

1—cap cover with horn 带有喇叭按钮罩盖；2—nut 螺母；3—washer 垫圈；4—steering wheel 转向盘；5—fixed bolt for steering post switch 转向柱开关的固定螺栓；6—steering signal light switch 转向信号灯开关；7—wiper switch 刮水器开关；8—upper shield cover 上护罩；9—lower shield cover 下护罩；10—sleeve 套管；11—steering shaft 转向轴；12—anchor ring 支撑环；13—steering lock housing 转向锁外壳；14—steering lock 转向锁；15—ignition switch 点火开关；16—lock core 锁心；17—spring 弹簧；18—multi gear joint shaft sleeve 多齿接头轴套

## Reading Materials

### The Electrical System

The electrical system does several jobs. It cranks the engine for starting. It supplies the high-voltage that ignite the compressed air-fuel mixture in the combustion chambers. It includes the battery, generator, starting system, ignition system, light system, horn system, radio and other devices.

#### Battery

The purpose of battery is to supply current for operation of the cranking motor and the ignition system when the engine is being cranked for starting. It also supplies current for light, radio, and other electrical accessories at times when the generator is not operating fast enough to handle the electrical load. The amount of current the battery can supply is strictly limited by the "capacity" of the battery, which in turn depends on the amount of chemicals it contains.

When we make a battery, several similar plates are properly spaced and welded to form a plate group. Plates of two types are used, one for the positive plate group, the other for the negative plate group. A positive plate is nested with a negative plate group, with separators placed between the plates. Separators are designed to hold the plates apart so that they do not touch, and at the same time they must be porous enough to permit liquid to circulate between the plates. The liquid, called the electrolyte, is made up of about 40 percent sulfuric acid and about 60 percent water. When sulfuric acid is placed between the plates, chemical actions take place that remove electrons one group of plates and mass them at the other.

#### Generator

Generator is a device that converts mechanical energy from the automobile engine into a flow of electric current. The generator replaces in the battery the current used after starting the engine and also supplies current for operation of electrical devices, such as the ignition system, lights, radio, and so on. The generator is usually mounted on the side of the engine block. It is driven by the engine belt.

For many years, all automotive generators were direct-current(d-c)units. In recent years, alternating-current(a-c)generators, or alternator, as they are so called, have come into widespread use. Direct-current flows in one direction only. Alternating current flows first in one direction and then in the other. The a-c generator, or alternator, produces alternation current. The battery, ignition system, and other electrical components on the automobile cannot use a-c, however, they are all d-c units. The a-c output must therefore be rectified, or changed to d-c.

# Unit 16  AUTOMOBILE ELECTRICAL SYSTEM

Many charging circuits use an indicator lamp to indicate whether or not the alternator is charging the battery.

An ammeter is used on many cars. It provides a better idea to the driver of what is happening in the charging circuit. The ammeter shows in a general way how much current is flowing to the battery during charge, and how much is flowing from the battery if the alternator is not charging the battery.

Seat Adjusters

Electric seat adjusters are used on front seats to adjust the seat height, position, and tilt. The adjuster that moves the seat up and down and from front to rear is called a four-way adjuster. The adjuster includes a driver motor, a transmission, drive cables, slides, tracks, and supports and so on.

Window Regulators

A power window regulator has an electric motor which is mounted in the lower part of the door. It drives a rack and levers, which raise or lower the window.

阅读材料（参考译文）

## 电 气 系 统

电气系统可以实现多种功能，包括转动起动机从而起动发动机。它提供高压点燃燃烧室内压缩混合气。它包括蓄电池、发电机、起动系统、点火系统、灯光系统、喇叭系统、收音机和其他设备。

【参考视频】

### 蓄电池

蓄电池的目的是当发动机起动时为起动机或点火系统提供电流，同时当发电机不能满足负载时也为灯光、其他电气附件提供电流。蓄电池提供电流的数量受蓄电池容量的限制，取决于电池包含化学物质的数量。

【参考视频】

我们在制作蓄电池时，将几块相似的极板正确布置并焊接从而形成极板组。有两种类型极板：一个是正极板组，另一个是负极板组，正极板组和负极板组相互嵌套安装，中间有隔板。隔板将极板隔开防止接触，同时必须让电解液在极板间能够循环流通。蓄电池电解液由40%硫酸和60%纯净水组成，当电解液放入极板间时发生化学反应，这种化学反应使电子从一个极板组向另一极板组集中。

### 发电机

发电机是一个将发动机的机械能转变为电能的设备。在发动机起动后发电机取代蓄电池电流并且为电气设备运行提供电流，如点火系统、灯光系统、收音机等。发电机安装在发动机机体一侧，并且通过传动带由发动机驱动。

【参考视频】

多年来，所有汽车发电机都是直流单元。近年来，交流发电机被广泛使用。直流电的电流仅仅向一个方向流动，而交流电首先向一个方向流动然后向另一个方向流动。交流发电机产生方向交替的电流，然而汽车上的蓄电池、点火系统和电气设备不能用交流电，它们都是直流单元，所以交流输出必须被整流或转变为直流电。

许多充电电路使用一个指示灯，用来指示交流发电机是否向蓄电池充电。

许多轿车上常使用电流表，它可以告诉驾驶员充电电路工作是否正常。通常情况下，从电流表可以看出蓄电池充电的多少，并且在交流发电机不给蓄电池充电情况下可以看出蓄电池对外提供电流的多少。

**座椅调节器**

电控座椅调节器用在前排座椅，用于调节座椅高度、位置和倾斜度。可以让座椅上下和前后进行运动的调节器称为四方向调节器，这种调节器包括一个驱动电动机、动力传递装置、驱动线路、滑条、轨道和支架等。

**门窗调节器**

动力门窗调节器有一个电控电动机，该电控电动机安装在门窗的下部，驱动齿条和丝杠，从而升起或降低门窗。

# Unit 17

# AUTOMOBILE AIR CONDITIONING SYSTEM
# 汽车空调系统

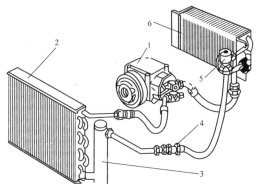

图 17.1  Air conditioner system  汽车空调系统
1—compressor 压缩机；2—condenser 冷凝器；3—receiver 储液干燥器；4—sight glass 视液窗；5—expansion valve 膨胀阀；6—evaporator 蒸发器

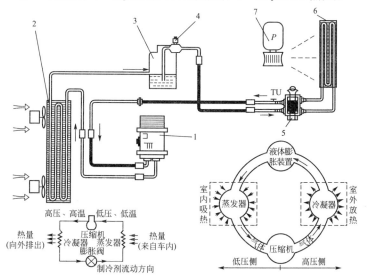

图 17.2  Air conditioning system(schematic)  汽车空调系统的工作原理
1—compressor 压缩机；2—condenser 冷凝器；3—receiver 储液干燥器；4—relief valve 压力安全阀；5—expansion valve 膨胀阀；6—evaporator 蒸发器；7—blower 鼓风机

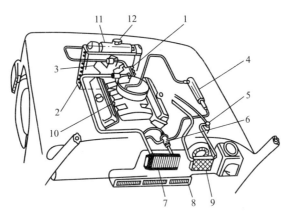

图 17.3　Car air conditioner layout　轿车空调的布置

1—compressor 压缩机；2—condenser 冷凝器；3—condenser fan 冷凝器风扇；4—drier filter 干燥过滤器；5—hot water valve 热水阀；6—expansion valve 膨胀阀；7—evaporator 蒸发器；8—cooling grille 冷风送风格栅；9—heating grille 热风送风格栅；10—engine 发动机；11—radiator 散热器；12—radiator cap 散热器盖

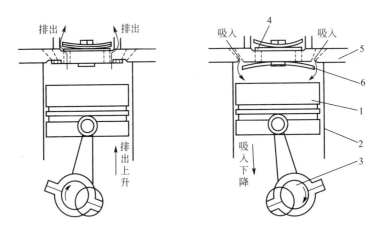

图 17.4　Crankshaft link compressor　曲轴连杆式压缩机

1—piston 活塞；2—cylinder 气缸；3—crankshaft link 曲轴连杆；4—exhaust valve 排气阀；5—valve plate 阀板；6—inlet valve 进气阀

# Unit 17　AUTOMOBILE AIR CONDITIONING SYSTEM

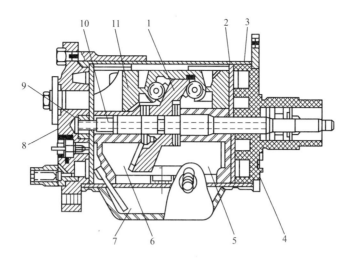

图 17.5　Wobble plate type compressor　斜盘式压缩机

1—wobble plate 斜盘；2—intake valve 进气阀；3—exhaust valve 排气阀；
4—front cap 前盖；5—front cylinder 前气缸；6—back cylinder 后气缸；
7—bottom case 油底壳；8—back cap 后盖；9—oil pump gear
机油泵齿轮；10—main shaft 主轴；11—piston 活塞

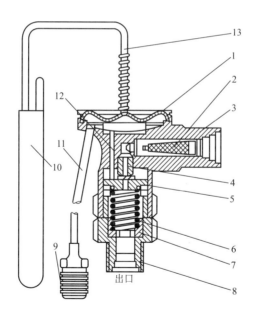

图 17.6　Outer balance expansion valve　外平衡膨胀阀

1—diaphragm 膜片；2—filter pads 滤网；3—valve housing 阀体；4—orifice 节
流孔；5—valve core 阀芯；6—overheating spring 过热弹簧；7—spring seat
弹簧座；8—spring adjusting nut 弹簧调节螺母；9—outer balance
pipe joint 外平衡管接口（蒸发器出口歧管）；10—remote
bulb 感温包；11—outer balance pipe 外平衡管；
12—pin 顶杆；13—capillary tube 毛细管

【参考视频】

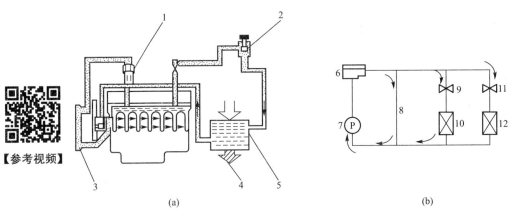

图 17.7　The schematic diagram of hot water heating system　热水式采暖系统示意图

（a）the schematic diagram of system 系统示意图；（b）the schematic diagram of pipeline 管路示意图

1—water tank thermostat 水箱恒温器；2、11—hot water valve 热水阀；3—water tank 水箱；4—heated wind 暖风；5、12—heat exchanger 热交换器；6—engine 发动机；7—water pump 水泵；8—by-pass pipeline 旁通管路；9—thermostat 恒温器；10—radiator 散热器

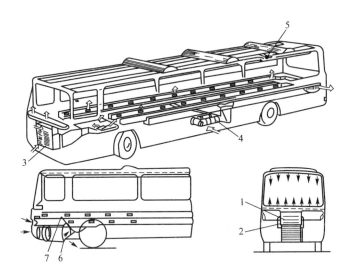

图 17.8　Bus heater system　大客车暖气系统

1—wind-window glass heater 风窗玻璃加热器；2—valve 阀；3—radiator 散热器；4—heating units 暖风装置；5—heating pipe 暖风管；6—damper 空气门；7—damper position adjustor 空气门位置调节器

# Unit 17  AUTOMOBILE AIR CONDITIONING SYSTEM

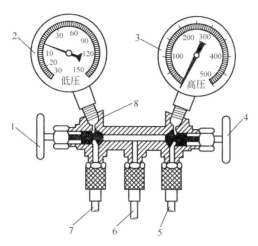

图 17.9  Manifold press  歧管压力表

1—low pressure hand valve 低压手动阀(LO); 2—low pressure gauge(blue)低压表(蓝); 3—high pressure gauge(red)高压表(红); 4—high pressure hand valve(h)高压手动阀(H); 5—high pressure slide pipe(red)高压侧软管(红); 6—service soft pipe(green)维修用软管(绿); 7—low pressure slide soft pipe(blue)低压侧软管(蓝); 8—manifold seat 歧管座

## Reading Materials

### Air Conditioning System

Vehicles have primarily three different types of air conditioning systems. While each of the three types differs, the concept and design are very similar to one another. The most common components which make up these automotive systems are the following: compressor, condenser, evaporator, expansion valve, and receiver-drier, etc.

#### Compressor

Commonly referred to as the heart of the system, the compressor is a belt driven pump that is fastened to the engine. It is responsible for compressing refrigerant gas.

The A/C system is spilt into two sides, a high pressure side and a low pressure side. Since the compressor is basically a pump, it must have an inside and a discharge side. The intake side draws in refrigerant gas from the outlet of the evaporator.

Once the refrigerant is drawn into the suction side, it is compressed and sent to the condenser, where it can then transfer the heat that is absorbed from the inside of the vehicle.

#### Condenser

The condenser has much the same appearance as the radiator in the car since the two have very similar functions. The condenser is designed to radiate heat. Its location is usually in front of the radiator, but in some cases, due to aerodynamic improvements to the body of a vehicle, its location may differ. Condensers must have good airflow anytime the system is in operation. On rear wheel drive vehicles, this is usually accomplished by taking advantage of your existing engine's cooling fan. On front wheel drive vehicles, condenser airflow is supplemented with one or more electric cooling fans.

As hot compressed gases are introduced into the top of the condenser, they are cooled off. As the gas cools, it condenses and goes out of the bottom of the condenser as a high-pressure liquid.

### Evaporator

Located inside the vehicle, the evaporator serves as the heat absorption component. The evaporator provides several functions. Its primary duty is to remove heat from the inside of your vehicle. A secondary benefit is dehumidification. As warmer air travels through the aluminum fins of the cooler evaporator coil, the moisture contained in the air condenses on its surface. Dust and pollen passing through the evaporator stick to its wet surfaces and drain off to the outside at last. On humid days you may have seen this as water dripping from the bottom of your vehicle.

### Thermal Expansion Valve

Another common refrigerant regulator is the thermal expansion valve. This type of valve can sense both temperature and pressure, and is very efficient at regulating refrigerant flow to the evaporator. Several variations of this valve are commonly found. One of a thermal expansion valve is "H block" type. This type of valve is usually located at the firewall, between the evaporator inlet and outlet tubes.

### Receiver-drier

The receiver-drier is used on the high side of systems that use a thermal expansion valve. This type of metering valve requires liquid refrigerant. To ensure that the valve gets liquid refrigerant, a receiver is used. The primary function of the receiver-drier is to separate gas and liquid. The secondly purpose is to remove moisture and filter out dirt.

阅读材料（参考译文）

【参考视频】

空 调 系 统

汽车主要有三种不同类型的空调系统，虽然每种系统各有不同，但其概念和设计是非常相似的。通常这些系统包括以下组件：压缩机、冷凝器、蒸发器、膨胀阀和储液干燥器等。

**压缩机**

压缩机是空调系统的核心，由一个驱动泵通过一根传动带和发动机紧固在一起。它负责压缩制冷剂。

## Unit 17　AUTOMOBILE AIR CONDITIONING SYSTEM

空调系统分为两侧，高压侧和低压侧。因为压缩机大体上是一个泵，所以必须有输入端和输出端。进气侧吸入从蒸发器出来的制冷剂气体。

一旦制冷剂被压缩机进气侧吸入，它将被压缩并送入冷凝器，冷凝器将制冷剂从车内吸收的热量散去。

### 冷凝器

冷凝器和散热器有非常相似的功能，因此从外表看它们也非常相似。冷凝器用来散发热量，经常布置在散热器的前面，但是在某些情况下由于车体空气动力学的改进，它们在车上布置的位置也不同。冷凝器在工作时必须有好的空气流通，在后轮驱动的车辆上，冷凝器通常由发动机冷却风扇驱动，在前轮驱动的车辆上，冷凝器由一个或更多的电控风扇驱动。

当热的压缩气体从冷凝器的上端进入时很快就被冷却，并且变成高压液体从冷凝器底部流出。

### 蒸发器

蒸发器装在车内，负责吸收车内热量。蒸发器有多个功能，其中主要的任务是吸收车内的热量，另外还能除去车内的湿气。当热的空气流过蒸发器铝制网上时，空气中的湿气凝结在蒸发器表面。灰尘和花粉通过蒸发器时被吸附在蒸发器表面并且最终会排到外界。在潮湿的天气你会看到这些湿气会变成水从汽车底部流出。

### 热膨胀阀

另外一个制冷剂调节器是热膨胀阀，这种阀可以感受温度和压力，并且能高效率地控制制冷剂流向蒸发器的流量。这种阀有几种不同的类型，其中一个是H形膨胀阀，这种阀经常安装蒸发器的入口管路和出口管路之间。

### 储液干燥器

储液干燥器用在装有热膨胀阀冷却系统的高压侧。热膨胀阀要求吸入的是液态制冷剂，为了确保吸入的是液态制冷剂，必须采用储液干燥器。储液干燥器的主要功能是分离气体和液体，第二个目的是除去湿气和过滤灰尘。

# Unit 18

# AUTOMOBILE REPAIR TOOLS AND EQUIPMENTS
# 汽车维修工具和设备

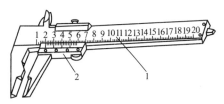

图 18.1  Vernier calliper  游标卡尺
1—rule body 尺身；2—vernier 游标

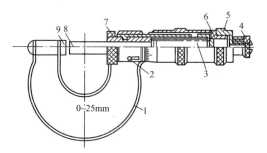

图 18.2  Outside micrometer  外径千分尺
1—frame 尺架；2—clamp equipment 锁紧装置；3、8—spindle 测微螺杆；4—ratchet 棘轮；5—nut 螺母；6—thimble 微分筒；7—fixing sleeve 固定套筒；9—anvil 测砧

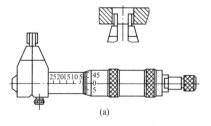
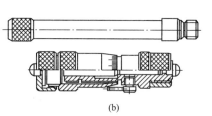

图 18.3  Inside micrometer  内径千分尺
(a) general inside micro meter 普通型内径千分尺；
(b) rod inside micro meter 杆式内径千分尺

# Unit 18 AUTOMOBILE REPAIR TOOLS AND EQUIPMENTS

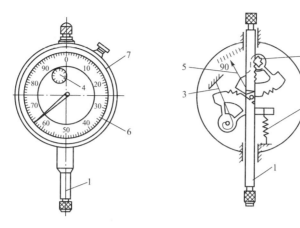

图 18.4 Dial indicator structure 百分表的结构
1—measuring rod 测杆；2—return spring 回位弹簧；3、4—short pointer 短指针；
5—long pointer 长指针；6—active indicator panel 活动表盘；7—indicator shell 表壳

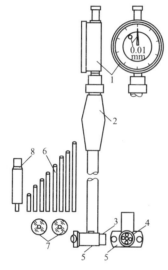

图 18.5 Cylinder gauge 量缸表
1—dial indicator 百分表；2—indicator rod 表杆；
3—connecting rod base 连杆座；4—active
test rod 活动测杆；5—supporting shelf
支撑架；6—connecting rod 连杆；
7—fixing nut 固定螺母；8—extension
connecting rod 加长接杆

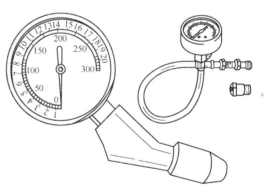

图 18.6 Cylinder pressure gauge 气缸压力表

图 18.7 Cylinder leakage detection meter
气缸漏气量检测仪

图 18.8 Crankcase leakage tester
曲轴箱窜气测量仪

图 18.9　Vacuum gauge　真空表

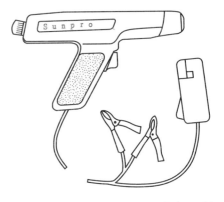
图 18.10　Ignition timing light　点火正时灯

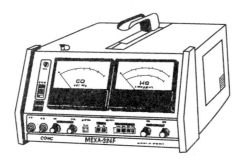
图 18.11　Engine waste gas analyzer　发动机废气分析仪

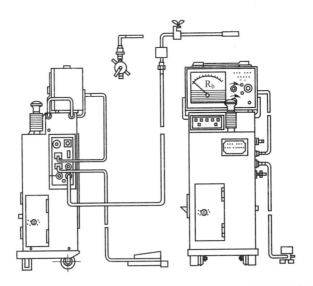
图 18.12　Semi-automatic exhaust smoke measurement　半自动排气烟度计

# Unit 18  AUTOMOBILE REPAIR TOOLS AND EQUIPMENTS

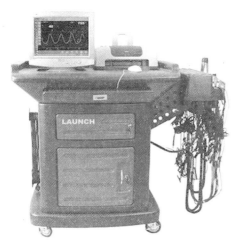

图 18.13  Engine analyzer  发动机分析仪

图 18.14  Chassis dynamometer  底盘测功机

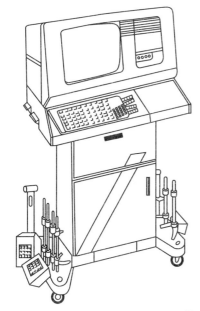

图 18.15  Four-wheel locating instrument  四轮定位仪

图 18.16  Chassis gap tester  底盘间隙检测仪

图 18.17  Braking test stand  制动试验台

图 18.18  Automobile sideslip test stand
汽车侧滑试验台

图 18.19  Digital universal meter
数字万用表

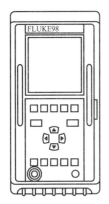
图 18.20　Automobile universal oscilloscope
汽车万用示波器

图 18.21　Automobile universal decoder
汽车解码器

图 18.22　Injector washer　喷油器清洗机

图 18.23　Injection pump test stand　喷油泵试验台

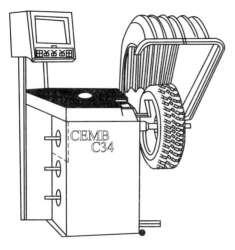
图 18.24　Tyre balance machine　轮胎平衡机

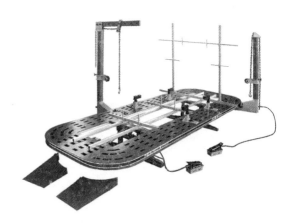
图 18.25　Chassis straightener　底盘校正仪

## Unit 18　AUTOMOBILE REPAIR TOOLS AND EQUIPMENTS

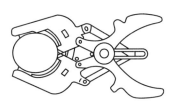

图 18.26　Piston ring disassembling pliers
活塞环拆装钳

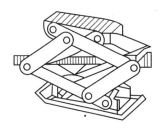

图 18.27　Lifting machine　举升机

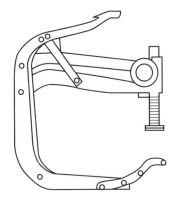

图 18.28　Valve disassembling pliers　气门拆装钳

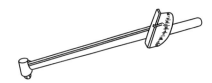

图 18.29　Torque wrench　扭力扳手

## Reading Materials

### Automobile Repair Tools and Equipments

Automotive fault diagnostic equipments can enlarge the perception of the automotive maintenance personnel capacity. Some equipments have common vehicle technical data, which will help improving the accuracy of technical state judgment for automotive maintenance personnel, and then some equipments have certain ability to analyze and judge, in order to achieve automotive failures fast, accurate and effective diagnosis of providing technical support. Automobile maintenance equipments can effectively improve the productivity of vehicle maintenance and repair quality.

Auto fault diagnostic equipments mainly include engine, chassis and electric control system.

### Engine Fault Diagnostic Equipments

They include cylinder pressure gauge, cylinder leakage detection meter, crankcase leakage tester, vacuum gauge, ignition timing light, engine waste gas analyzer, exhaust smoke measurement, engine analyzer.

### Chassis Fault Diagnostic Equipments

They include chassis dynamometer, four-wheel locating instrument, chassis gap tester, braking test stand, automobile sideslip test stand.

### Electronic Control Fault Diagnostic System

They mainly include digital universal meter, automobile universal oscilloscope, automobile decoder.

阅读材料（参考译文）

## 汽车维修工具和设备

汽车故障诊断设备能帮助我们提高汽车维修的能力，一些设备有车载终端数据，这些数据可以提高我们对汽车故障判断的准确性，并且有些设备自身有分析判断的能力，可以为快速、准确和高效地诊断汽车故障提供技术支持。汽车维修设备可以有效地提高车辆维护和修理的质量。

汽车故障诊断设备主要包括诊断发动机、底盘和电控系统的设备。

### 发动机故障诊断设备

发动机故障诊断设备包括气缸压力表、气缸漏气检测仪、曲轴箱窜气检测仪、真空表、点火正时灯、发动机废气分析仪、排气烟度检测和发动机分析仪。

### 底盘故障诊断设备

底盘故障诊断设备包括底盘测功机、四轮定位仪、底盘间隙检测仪、制动试验台和汽车侧滑试验台。

### 电控系统故障诊断设备

电控系统故障诊断设备主要包括数字万用表、汽车示波器和汽车解码器。

汽车维修工具，一般指用于手工操作的各类维修工具，如螺丝刀、扳手、气动工具、套筒工具、工具车、工具箱、工作台等。

【参考视频】

【参考视频】

【参考视频】

【参考视频】

【参考视频】

## Unit 18　AUTOMOBILE REPAIR TOOLS AND EQUIPMENTS

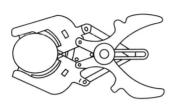

图 18.26　Piston ring disassembling pliers
活塞环拆装钳

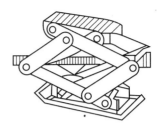

图 18.27　Lifting machine　举升机

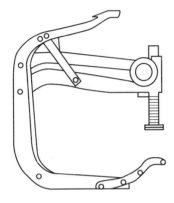

图 18.28　Valve disassembling pliers　气门拆装钳

图 18.29　Torque wrench　扭力扳手

Reading Materials

### Automobile Repair Tools and Equipments

Automotive fault diagnostic equipments can enlarge the perception of the automotive maintenance personnel capacity. Some equipments have common vehicle technical data, which will help improving the accuracy of technical state judgment for automotive maintenance personnel, and then some equipments have certain ability to analyze and judge, in order to achieve automotive failures fast, accurate and effective diagnosis of providing technical support. Automobile maintenance equipments can effectively improve the productivity of vehicle maintenance and repair quality.

Auto fault diagnostic equipments mainly include engine, chassis and electric control system.

### Engine Fault Diagnostic Equipments

They include cylinder pressure gauge, cylinder leakage detection meter, crankcase leakage tester, vacuum gauge, ignition timing light, engine waste gas analyzer, exhaust smoke measurement, engine analyzer.

**Chassis Fault Diagnostic Equipments**

They include chassis dynamometer, four-wheel locating instrument, chassis gap tester, braking test stand, automobile sideslip test stand.

**Electronic Control Fault Diagnostic System**

They mainly include digital universal meter, automobile universal oscilloscope, automobile decoder.

 阅读材料（参考译文）

### 汽车维修工具和设备

汽车故障诊断设备能帮助我们提高汽车维修的能力，一些设备有车载终端数据，这些数据可以提高我们对汽车故障判断的准确性，并且有些设备自身有分析判断的能力，可以为快速、准确和高效地诊断汽车故障提供技术支持。汽车维修设备可以有效地提高车辆维护和修理的质量。

汽车故障诊断设备主要包括诊断发动机、底盘和电控系统的设备。

**发动机故障诊断设备**

发动机故障诊断设备包括气缸压力表、气缸漏气检测仪、曲轴箱窜气检测仪、真空表、点火正时灯、发动机废气分析仪、排气烟度检测和发动机分析仪。

**底盘故障诊断设备**

底盘故障诊断设备包括底盘测功机、四轮定位仪、底盘间隙检测仪、制动试验台和汽车侧滑试验台。

**电控系统故障诊断设备**

电控系统故障诊断设备主要包括数字万用表、汽车示波器和汽车解码器。

汽车维修工具，一般指用于手工操作的各类维修工具，如螺丝刀、扳手、气动工具、套筒工具、工具车、工具箱、工作台等。

【参考视频】　【参考视频】　【参考视频】　【参考视频】　【参考视频】

## 附录 A

# 汽车专业词汇（英—汉）

## A

absorber 减振器
acceleration sensor 加速传感器
accommodate 容纳
accumulator 蓄电池，蓄压器
activate 驱动，激发
additive 附加的，添加的
adjusting washer 调整垫片
adjustment 调整
admission 进入，进气
adjusting screw 调整螺钉
adjusting cable 调整拉索
adjusting plug 调整盖
adjusting screw assembly 调整螺栓总成
adjusting washer 调整垫片
adjusting, diff. bearing 差速器轴承调整螺母
adjustment system 调节装置
agent 试剂
air brakes 空气制动
air-cooled 风冷的
air-conditioner compressor 空调压缩机
air filter, air cleaner 空气滤清器
air-flow sensor 空气流量传感器

air-fuel mixture 空气燃油混合气
air-fuel ratio 空气燃油混合比
air gap 间隙
air-reserve tank 储气筒
air spring 空气弹簧
air supply system 空气供给系统
air suspension 空气悬架
air cleaner assembly 空气滤清器总成
air cleaner cartridge 空气滤清器滤芯
air compressor 空气压缩机
air condition compressor 空调压缩机
alternator 交流发电机
anti-lock brake system 防抱死制动系统
antifreeze compounds 防冻剂
armature 电枢
articulate 用关节连接，接合
automatic transmission 自动变速器
automatic transmission fluid 自动变速器油
automobile 汽车
axle 车轴
axle bearing 车轴轴承

## B

badge 车标
baffle plate 导流板
balance weight 平衡配重
ball bearing 球轴承
ball joint 球接头
barrel （化油器）腔，套筒，柱塞套
battery 蓄电池
battery voltage 蓄电池电压
beam 梁、横梁
bearing 轴承
bearing cap 轴承盖
bevel 锥齿轮，斜齿
blade 刮水器刮片，叶片
bleeding 放气
blind hole 盲孔
block 气缸

blow-by 窜漏
bolt 螺栓
boost 增压
bore 缸径
brake drum 制动鼓
brake fluid 制动液
brake horsepower 制动马力
brake hose 制动软管
brake lights 制动灯
brake light switch 制动灯开关
brake line 制动油管
brake pedal 制动踏板
brake shoe 制动蹄片
butterfly valve 节流阀、节气门
bypass hose 旁通管

## C

cable harness 电线束
cam bearing 凸轮轴轴承
cam plate 凸轮盘
cam set assembly 凸轮总成
camber 车轮外倾角
camshaft 凸轮轴
camshaft sensor 凸轮轴位置传感器
camshaft sprocket 凸轮轴链轮
camshaft timing gear 凸轮轴正时齿轮
carburetor 化油器
centrifugal advance mechanism 离心点火提前机构
chain 链（条）
chamber 室，腔
charcoal canister 活性炭罐
charger 充电器
chassis 底盘
check valve 单向阀

circuit 电路
clearance 间隙
clutch 离合器
clutch disc 离合器片
clutch fork 离合器拨叉
clutch input shaft 离合器输入轴
clutch pedal 离合器踏板
clutch pedal free travel 离合器踏板自由间隙
clutch pressure plate 离合器压板
clutch shaft 离合器轴
coil 线圈
coil spring 螺旋弹簧
cold-start 冷车起动
cold-start valve 冷起动阀
column 圆柱，杆
combustion 燃烧
combustion chamber 燃烧室

combustion pressure 燃烧压力
component 组件
compressor 压缩机
computer-aided technology 计算机辅助技术
condense 凝结
condenser 冷凝器
configuration 构造、结构
connecting-rod 连杆
connecting-rod bearing 连杆轴承
connecting-rod bolt 连杆轴承螺栓
connecting-rod cap 连杆轴承盖
control pulse 控制脉冲
control collar （油量）控制滑套
control rack 控制齿条
control sleeve 控制套筒
coolant 冷却液
coolant control engine vacuum switch 温控真空开关
coolant gallery 冷却液道
coolant temperature indicator 冷却液温度指示表
coolant temperature sensor 冷却液温度传感器
cooling fins 散热片
corrosion 腐蚀
counterbalance 平衡力
counterweight 平衡重
cowl 前围板
crank case 曲轴箱
crank pin 曲柄销
crankshaft 曲轴
crankshaft main bearing 曲轴主轴承
crankshaft sensor 曲轴位置传感器
crankshaft timing gear 曲轴正时齿轮
cross member 横梁
cursor 指针
cushion 软垫，坐垫
cycle 循环
cylinder 气缸
cylinder head 气缸盖
cylinder head screw 气缸盖螺钉
cylinder liner 气缸套
cylinder wall 气缸壁

D

damper 阻尼器，减振器
dashboard 仪表板
delivery quantity 供油量
delivery valve 出油阀
delivery valve and valve seat assembly 出油阀与阀座总成
detonation control system 爆燃控制系统
diagnose 诊断
diesel engine 柴油发动机
differential case 差速器壳
displacement 排量
disk brake 盘式制动器
distributorless ignition system 无分电器点火系统
distributor pump 分配泵
driving axle 驱动轴，驱动桥
drum 制动鼓
dram brake 鼓式制动器

E

EGR control valve EGR 控制阀
EGR delay solenoid EGR 延迟线圈
EGR temperature valve EGR 温控阀
electrical system 电气系统
electromagnetic 电磁的
electronic control unit(ECU) 电子控制单元

electronic fan　电动风扇
electronic ignition system　电子点火系统
electronic spark timing(EST)　电子点火正时
electric fuel pump　电动汽油泵
eliminate　消除，除去
emission control system　废气控制系统
engine block　发动机缸体
evaporative emission control(EEC)　汽油蒸气控制系统
exhaust camshaft　排气门凸轮轴
exhaust emission，exhaust gases　废气
exhaust gas recirculation(EGR)　废气再循环系统
exhaust manifolds　排气歧管
exhaust stroke　排气行程
exhaust valve　排气门

## F

fabricate　制造
fahrenheit　华氏温度计
fan belt　风扇传动带
fan clutch　风扇离合器
fan shroud　风扇导风圈
fault　故障
fault diagnosis　故障诊断
filter　滤清器
flexible　柔韧的，灵活的
flexible connection　柔性连接
fluid coupling device　液力耦合装置
flywheel　飞轮
four-stroke-cycle engine　四冲程发动机
four wheel steering　四轮转向
frame　车架
friction disk　摩擦片，离合器片
friction horsepower　摩擦马力
front oil seal　前油封
front suspension　前悬架
front-wheel alignment　前轮校正
front-wheel drive　前轮驱动
fuel　燃油
fuel deliver　供油
fuel filter　燃油滤清器
fuel metering system　燃油计量系统
fuel pump　燃油泵
fuel pump gasket　燃油泵垫片
fuel rail　燃油分供管
fuel-system　燃油系统
fuel supply system　燃油供给系统
fuel-tank　油箱
fuel-tank cap　油箱盖
full-floating pin　全浮式活塞销
full-load　全负荷
function　功能，作用
fuse　熔丝

## G

gasket　垫圈，衬垫
gasoline engine　汽油发动机
gear　齿轮
gear box　齿轮箱
gear lubricating oil　齿轮润滑油
gear oil　齿轮油
gear oil pump　齿轮油泵
generator　发电机
governor　调速器
governor spring　离心式调速器弹簧
grille　护栅，格栅
groove　凹槽
gross brake horsepower（bhp）　总制动功率
ground　搭铁/接地

## H

hand-operated　手动操作的
head gasket　气缸垫
heater cote　加热器芯
heater hose　暖气水管
heat transfer process　传热过程
helical　螺旋状的
high pressure line　高压油管
high-pressure solenoid　高压电磁阀
high-voltage surge　高压电

hole type nozzle　多孔式喷嘴
hood　发动机罩
horsepower　马力
hose　水管，橡皮油管
hub assembly　轮毂总成
hydraulic　液压的
hydraulic brake　液压制动
hydraulic brake booster　液压制动增压器
hydraulic valve lifter　液压式气门挺柱

## I

idle　怠速
ignite　点火，点燃
ignition coil　点火线圈
ignition distribution　点火分电器
ignition module　点火模块
ignition signal　点火信号
ignition timing　点火正时
impeller　泵轮，叶轮
inhibitor　[化]抑制剂，防腐剂
initiate　开始，发动
inject　喷射
injected fuel quantity　喷油量

injection nozzle　喷油嘴
injection timing advancer　喷油正时提前器
injector　喷油器
intake　入口，进口
intake air temperature sensor　进气温度传感器
intake manifolds　进气歧管
intake port　进气门孔
intake stroke　进气行程
intake valve　进气门
internal-combustion engine　内燃机

## J

jack　千斤顶
jet　喷口，喷嘴
journal　轴颈

jump　跳线
jumper wire　跨接线

## K

king pin　轴向节销
knock sensor　爆燃传感器

knuckle　关节杆

## L

lateral tie bar　横向推力杆

lead　铅

leaf spring 叶片弹簧
leak 漏，泄漏
leakage 漏，泄漏
leakage return pipe 回油管
lighting circuit 照明电路
liner 衬垫
liquid-cooled 水冷的
liquid-vapor separator 液体油气分离器
loading room 货箱
lobe 凸缘
locating lug, locking lip 定位凸缘
lubricating oil 润滑油
lubrication 润滑

## M

magnetic 磁的，有磁性的
magnetic coil 电磁线圈
magnetic field 磁场
main-bearing 主轴承
main-bearing journals 主轴颈
main gallery 主油道
manifold 歧管
manifold vacuum 歧管真空
manual 手动的，手工的
manual transmission 手动变速器
mechanical governor 机械式调速器
mechanism 机械装置
mesh 啮合
mixture 混合物
mode 方式，模式
monitor 监控器
motor vehicle 机动车辆

## N

needle 针
needle bearing 针状轴承
neutral 空挡
nozzle 喷嘴
nozzle holder 喷油器体
nozzle needle and the nozzle 针阀与针阀体
nut 螺母

## O

offset weight 平衡重
OHC 顶置凸轮轴式
oil-control ring 油环
oil filter 机油滤清器
oil level gauge, oil dipstick 机油量尺
oil pan 油底盘
oil pan drain plug 油底盘放油塞
oil-returning slot 回油槽
oil slinger 挡油圈
open and close-loop 开环与闭环
operating conditions 运行状况，工况
operating temperature 运行温度，工作温度
output shaft 输出轴
overdrive 超速传动
overhaul 彻底检查，大修
overheating 过热
oxidize （使）氧化
oxygen 氧气
oxygen sensor 氧传感器

## P

panel 仪表板
pedal 踏板
performance 性能
pin 销，针
pinion 小齿轮
pintle nozzle 轴针式喷嘴
parking brake 驻车制动
piston 活塞
piston and rod assembly 活塞连杆总成
piston head 活塞顶
piston pin 活塞销
piston rings 活塞环
piston skirt 活塞裙部
plunger 柱塞
plunger lift 柱塞升程
plunger return spring 柱塞回位弹簧
plunger and barrel assembly 柱塞，套筒偶件
poppet valve 气门
port 端口，通道

power steering 动力转向
power steering pump 动力转向机油压泵
power stroke 做功行程
power train 动力传动机构
precombustion chamber 预燃烧室
pressure regulator 压力调节器
primary circuit 低压电路
principle 原理
printed circuit 印制电路
process 过程，进程
propel 推进，驱动
propeller shaft 传动轴
proportioning valve 比例阀
protrude 伸出
pulley 带盘
push-rod 推杆
pulse 脉冲
push out 排出

## R

rack and pinion steering 齿条式转向
radial tire 辐射状轮胎，子午线轮胎
radiator 散热器
radiator cap 散热器盖
radiator overflow hose 散热器溢水管
radiator pressure cap 压力式散热器盖
ratio 比，比率
rear axle 后轴
rear suspension 后悬架
rear-wheel drive 后轮驱动
reciprocating-piston engine 往复活塞式发动机
refrigerant 制冷剂
regulate 调节、校准
relief valve 泄压阀

removable 可拆装的，可更换的
retard 阻碍，制动
return spring 回位弹簧
reverse 倒挡，倒退
rib 加强肋
ring gap 活塞环开口间隙
ring groove 活塞环槽
ring land 活塞环岸
rocker arm 摇臂
rocker arm assembly 摇臂总成
rocker arm shaft 摇臂轴
rod big end 连杆大端
rod small end 连杆小端
rotor 分火头
rubber ring 橡皮水封

## S

scale 水垢
scavenge 扫气，排气
screw 螺钉，螺杆
screw driver 螺钉旋具
screw plug 螺塞
seal 密封
secondary circuit 高压电路
secondary injection(dribble) 二次喷射
sector 扇形齿轮
sensor 传感器
sheet 薄片
shifting 换挡
shift lever 变速杆
shock absorber 避振器
skirt 活塞裙
sleeve （阀）套
spark-advance control systems 点火提前控制系统
spark-advance mechanism 点火提前机构

spark plug 火花塞
spark-lug gap 火花塞间隙
spark-timing mark 点火正时记号
spindle 轴、杆
spline 齿条
spray 喷雾
spring retainer 弹簧座
sprocket 链轮齿，链轮
starter 起动机
starting motor 起动机
steering 操纵，转向
steering column 转向柱
steering drop arm 转向垂臂
steering wheel 转向盘
swirling 漩涡，涡流
switch 开关
switch on 接通
synthetic martial 合成材料

## T

tail pipe 排气管
tappet 挺杆
tensioner 张紧轮
terminate 停止，结束，终止
the basic duration of injection 基本喷射持续时间
thermal 热的，热量的
thermal efficiency 热效率
thermal insulation 热绝缘，绝热
thermostat 节温器
thermo-time switch 热时间开关
three-way catalytic converter 三元催化转换净化器
throttle valve 节气门
thrust 推力

timing chain 正时链条
timing gear cover 正时齿轮盖
timing light 正时灯
torque indicating wrench 扭矩指示扳手
torque tube 扭力管
torque wrench 扭力扳手
traction 牵引
transmission 变速器
transmission fluid 变速器润滑油
tread 胎面
trim 装饰
trunk （车尾的）行李箱
trunk lid 行李箱盖
tube 油管
turbine 涡轮

turbocharger 涡轮增压器
twist 扭曲

two-stroke-cycle engine 二冲程发动机

## U~V

uniformity 一致性
unitized-body construction 承载式车身结构，无车架车身结构
universal joint 万向节
upstroke 上行运动
vacuum 真空
vacuum advance 真空提前
vacuum advance mechanism 真空点火提前机构
valve 气门
valve guide 气门导管
valve head 气门头部
valve lifter 气门挺杆
valve operating clearance 气门间隙
valve port 气门孔
valve seat 气门座
valve spring 气门弹簧

valve stem 气门杆
valve timing 气门正时
valve-timing mark 气门正时记号
valve foot 气门脚
van 厢式货车
vane-type pump 叶片泵
vaporize （使）蒸发
variable compression ratio 可变压缩比
variable-displacement engine 可变排量式发动机
variable-valve-timing system 可变气门正时系统
vibration damper 扭力减振器
voltage 电压
volume 容积，体积
volumetric efficiency 容积效率

## W

wagon 货车
warm-air intake 热空气进气口
warm-up 暖车
washer 垫片
water pump 水泵
water jacket 水套
wear-indicators 磨损指示器
wear resistance 抗磨性
wheel 车轮
wheel alignment 车轮校正
wheel balance 车轮平衡

wheel base 轴距
wheel cylinder brake 制动分泵
wheel suspension 车轮悬架
windshield washer 风窗洗涤器
wiper blade 刮水器
wiper 刮水片
wiring harness 电线
worm gear sector 蜗轮齿机构，扇形齿轮
worm shaft 蜗杆轴
wrench 扳手

# 附录 B

# 汽车专业英语常见名词缩写

## A

| | | |
|---|---|---|
| AA | Automobile Association(UK) | 英国汽车协会 |
| AAA | American Automobile Association | 美国汽车协会 |
| AACV | auxiliary air control valve | 辅助空气控制阀 |
| AAP | auxiliary accelerating pump | 辅助加速泵 |
| AC | air conditioner | 空调 |
| ABS | antilock braking system | 防抱死制动系统 |
| ACS | air conditioning system | 空调系统 |
| ACL | air cleaner | 空气滤清器 |
| AEC | automotive emission control | 汽车排放控制 |
| AFC | air-fuel control | 空燃比调节装置 |
| AP | accelerator pedal | 加速踏板 |
| ARC | active fide control | 汽车平顺性自动控制 |
| ASR | acceleration slip regulation | 汽车驱动防滑控制系统 |
| AT | automatic transmission | 自动变速器 |
| ATF | automatic transmission fluid | 自动变速器油 |
| AVM | automatic vehicle monitoring | 车辆自动检测 |
| AWD | all-wheel drive | 全轮驱动 |
| AWP | awaiting parts | 维修备件 |
| AZS | automatic zero set | 自动调零 |

## B

| | | |
|---|---|---|
| BA | bore area | 气缸孔面积 |
| BAC | by-pass air control valve | 旁通空气阀 |
| BAS | brake assist system | 制动辅助系统 |
| BBW | brake by wire | 汽车电制动系统 |

# 附录B 汽车专业英语常见名词缩写

| BC | brake cylinder | 制动缸 |
| BDC | bottom dead center | 下止点 |
| BHP | brake horsepower | 制动马力 |
| BM | breakdown maintenance | 故障维修 |
| BP | best power | 最佳功率 |

## C

| CAD | computer-aided design | 计算机辅助设计 |
| CAM | computer aided manufacturing | 计算机辅助制造 |
| CAE | computer aided engineering | 计算机辅助工程 |
| CAP | crank angular position | 曲柄相位角 |
| CC | combustion chamber | 燃烧室 |
| CCC | computer command control | 计算机指令控制 |
| CCE | command control equipment | 指令控制装置 |
| CCS | cruise control system | 汽车巡航控制系统 |
| CIS | continuous injection system | 汽油连续喷射系统 |
| CMS | computer monitor system | 计算机监视系统 |
| CN | cetane number | 十六烷值 |
| CYL | cylindrical | 圆柱形的 |
| CVT | continuously variable transmission | 无级变速器 |

## D

| D | drive | 驱动 |
| DC | dead center | 止点 |
| DCI | direct cylinder injection | 直接喷入气缸 |
| DCV | deceleration control valve | 减速控制阀 |
| DFI | direct fuel injection | 直接燃油喷射 |
| DI | direction injection | 直接喷射 |
| DIS | direct ignition system | 无分电器点火系统 |
| DSC | dynamic stability controller | 动态稳定控制系统 |
| DSP | digtial signal processor | 数字信号处理器 |
| DTC | diagnostic trouble code | 故障诊断代码 |

## E

| EAC | engine air control | 发动机空气量控制 |
| EAS | electronic air suspension | 电子控制空气悬架 |
| EBA | electronic brake assist | 电子控制制动辅助 |
| EBD | electronic brake force distribution | 电子制动力分配系统配备 |

| | | |
|---|---|---|
| ECC | electronic control clutch | 电子控制离合器 |
| ECS | electronic controlled suspension | 电子控制悬架 |
| ECS | engine control system | 发动机控制系统 |
| ECT | emission control system | 电子控制自动变速系统 |
| ECU | electronic control unit | 电子控制单元 |
| EEC | engine electronic control center | 发动机电子控制中心 |
| EFI | electronic fuel injection | 电子燃油喷射 |
| EGR | exhaust gas recycle | 废气再循环 |
| EIS | electronic ignition system | 电子点火系统 |
| EPS | electric power steering | 电子助力转向系统 |
| ESP/DSC | electronic stability program | 电子车身稳定装置 |
| EIS | exhaust-gas turbo supercharge | 废气涡轮增压器 |

## F

| | | |
|---|---|---|
| F/A | fuel-air ratio | 空燃比 |
| F/R | front engine/rear wheel drive | 发动机前置后轮驱动 |
| FSI | fuel stratified injection | 燃料分层喷射技术 |

## G

| | | |
|---|---|---|
| GW | gross weight | 总质量 |
| GR | gear ratio | 传动比 |
| GPS | global position system | 全球定位系统 |

## H

| | | |
|---|---|---|
| HAS | heated air system | 空气加热系统 |
| H/D | heater/defroster | 加热器/除霜器 |
| HP | horsepower | 马力 |
| HTC | hydraulic torque convener | 液力变矩器 |

## I

| | | |
|---|---|---|
| IATS | intake air temperature sensor | 进气温度传感器 |
| IC | integrated circuit | 集成电路 |
| IDI | indirect injection | 间接喷射(非直喷式) |
| ISC | idle speed controller | 急速控制系统 |

## J

| | | |
|---|---|---|
| JAVC | jet air control valve | 空气喷射控制阀 |

## 附录B 汽车专业英语常见名词缩写

### K

| | | |
|---|---|---|
| KS | knock sensor | 爆燃传感器 |

### L

| | | |
|---|---|---|
| LC | load cell | 负荷传感器 |
| LEE | low emission engine | 低排放发动机 |
| LPG | liquefied petroleum gas | 液化石油气 |

### M

| | | |
|---|---|---|
| MAPS | manifold absolute pressure sensor | 进气歧管绝对压力传感器 |
| MATS | manifold air temperature sensor | 进气温度传感器 |
| MFI | multipoint fuel injection | 多点燃油喷射 |
| MIL | malfunction indicator lamp | 故障指示灯 |
| MIS | maintenance indicator system | 保养指示系统 |
| MSDI | multiple-spark discharge ignition | 多火花点火 |

### N

| | | |
|---|---|---|
| NA | naturally aspirated | 自然吸气 |
| NHP | nominal horsepower | 标定功率 |
| NT | net tons | 净重吨数 |

### O

| | | |
|---|---|---|
| OBC | on-board computer | 车载计算机 |
| OBD | on-board diagnostics | 车载诊断系统 |
| OC | oil consumption | 机油消耗量 |
| OCC | output circuit check | 输出电路检查 |
| OD | overdrive | 超速传动 |

### P

| | | |
|---|---|---|
| PAB | power-assisted brake | 助力制动 |
| PCV | positive crankcase ventilation | 曲轴箱强制通风 |
| PCM | power train control module | 动力系统控制模块 |
| PFI | port fuel injection(system) | 进气口燃油喷射(系统) |
| PPS | progressive power steering | 渐进式动力转向 |

### R

| | | |
|---|---|---|
| REGTS | recirculated exhaust gas temperature sensor | 废气再循环温度传感器 |

| | | |
|---|---|---|
| RPE | rotary piston engine | 转子活塞发动机 |
| R/R | rear engine/rear wheel drive | 发动机后置后轮驱动 |
| RWD | rear wheel drive | 后轮驱动 |

## S

| | | |
|---|---|---|
| SA | spark advance | 点火提前 |
| SAS | slow adjust screw | 慢车调整螺丝 |
| SCR | silicon controlled rectifier | 晶闸管整流器 |
| SCV | spark control valve | 点火控制阀 |
| SFI | sequential fuel injection | 顺序燃油喷射 |
| SGS | safe-guard system | 安全防护系统 |
| SMFI | sequential multipoint fuel injection | 顺序多点燃油喷射 |
| SOHC | single overhead camshaft | 单顶置凸轮轴 |
| SPI | single point injection | 单点喷射 |
| SRS | supplemental restraint system | 汽车安全气囊 |

## T

| | | |
|---|---|---|
| TAP | throttle angle position | 节气门开度位置 |
| TC | turbo charger | 涡轮增压器 |
| TCC | torque convener clutch | 液力变矩器 |
| TCI | transistorized coil ignition | 晶体管点火线圈 |
| TCS | traction control system | 循迹控制系统或牵引力控制系统 |
| TDC | top dead center | 上止点 |
| TDI | turbo charged direct injection | 涡轮增压直接喷射 |
| TPS | throttle position sensor | 节气门位置传感器 |

## U

| | | |
|---|---|---|
| UDC | upper dead center | 上止点 |
| U-joint | universal joint | 万向节 |

## V

| | | |
|---|---|---|
| VAB | variable air bleed | 可变空气量孔 |
| VCR | variable compression ratio | 可变压缩比 |
| VCV | vacuum control valve | 真空控制阀 |
| VIN | vehicle identification number | 机动车身份号码 |
| VIPS | variable induction port system | 可变进气口系统 |
| VSC | vehicle stability control | 汽车稳定控制系统 |

| | | |
|---|---|---|
| VTEC | variable valve timing and lift electronic control system | 可变气门正时及升程电子控制系统 |
| VVA | variable valve actuation | 可变气门驱动 |
| VVT | variable valve timing | 可变气门正时 |
| VVT-I | variable valve timing intelligent | 智能正时可变气门控制系统 |

## W

| | | |
|---|---|---|
| 4WD | four-wheel drive | 四轮驱动系统 |
| 4WS | four-wheel steer | 四轮转向系统 |
| WSS | wheel speed sensor | 轮速传感器 |

## X

| | | |
|---|---|---|
| X-Valve | expansion valve | 膨胀阀 |

## Y

| | | |
|---|---|---|
| YS | yield strength | 屈服强度 |

## Z

| | | |
|---|---|---|
| Z | zone | 区域 |

# 参 考 文 献

[1] 陈家瑞. 汽车构造 [M]. 3版. 北京：人民交通出版社，1994.
[2] 何宇漾. 汽车专业英语 [M]. 重庆：重庆大学出版社，2008.
[3] 范迪彬. 汽车构造 [M]. 合肥：安徽科学技术出版社，2001.
[4] 清华大学汽车工程系. 汽车构造 [M]. 北京：人民邮电出版社，2000.
[5] 郭新华. 汽车构造 [M]. 北京：高等教育出版社，2004.
[6] 王怡民. 汽车专业英语 [M]. 北京：人民交通出版社，2003.
[7] 胡宁. 现代汽车底盘构造 [M]. 上海：上海交通大学出版社，2003.
[8] 黄立新，等. 汽车专业英语 [M]. 西安：西安电子科技大学出版社，2006.
[9] 张为春. 汽车构造 [M]. 北京：机械工业出版社，2001.
[10] 周林福. 汽车底盘构造与维修 [M]. 北京：人民交通出版社，2002.
[11] 常明. 汽车底盘构造 [M]. 北京：国防工业出版社，2005.
[12] 李春明. 现代汽车底盘技术 [M]. 北京：北京理工大学出版社，2002.
[13] 吴文渊. 现代汽车电子控制技术 [M]. 北京：人民交通出版社，2002.
[14] 杜瑞丰，刘学武. 汽车底盘车身构造与修理 [M]. 北京：高等教育出版社，1996.
[15] 屠卫星. 汽车底盘构造与维修 [M]. 北京：人民交通出版社，2001.
[16] 李玉柱，罗新闻. 汽车专业英语 [M]. 北京：科学出版社，2007.
[17] 韩建保. 汽车实用英语 [M]. 北京：高等教育出版社，2005.
[18] 蔡伟义，虞兰. 汽车专业英语 [M]. 上海：上海交通大学出版社，2001.